CONTENTS

ADVISORY BOARD

HOW TO USE THIS BOOK

You have to know how to approach literature in order to get the most out of it. This *Barron's Book Notes* volume follows a plan based on methods used by some of the best students to read a work of literature.

Begin with the guide's section on the author's life and times. As you read, try to form a clear picture of the author's personality, circumstances, and motives for writing the work. This background usually will make it easier for you to hear the author's tone of voice, and follow where the author is heading.

Then go over the rest of the introductory material—such sections as those on the plot, characters, setting, themes, and style of the work. Underline, or write down in your notebook, particular things to watch for, such as contrasts between characters and repeated literary devices. At this point, you may want to develop a system of symbols to use in marking your text as you read. (Of course, you should only mark up a book you own, not one that belongs to another person or a school.) Perhaps you will want to use a different letter for each character's name, a different number for each major theme of the book, a different color for each important symbol or literary device. Be prepared to mark up the pages of your book as you read. Put your marks in the margins so you can find them again easily.

Now comes the moment you've been waiting for—the time to start reading the work of literature. You may want to put aside your *Barron's Book Notes* volume until you've read the work all the way through. Or you may want to alternate, reading the *Book Notes* analysis of each section as soon as you have finished reading the corresponding part of the original. Before you move on, reread crucial passages you don't fully understand. (Don't take this guide's analysis for granted—make up your own mind as to what the work means.)

Once you've finished the whole work of literature, you may want to review it right away, so you can firm up your ideas about what it means. You may want to leaf through the book concentrating on passages you marked in reference to one character or one theme. This is also a good time to reread the *Book Notes* introductory material, which pulls together insights on specific topics.

When it comes time to prepare for a test or to write a paper, you'll already have formed ideas about the work. You'll be able to go back through it, refreshing your memory as to the author's exact words and perspective, so that you can support your opinions with evidence drawn straight from the work. Patterns will emerge, and ideas will fall into place; your essay question or term paper will almost write itself. Give yourself a dry run with one of the sample tests in the guide. These tests present both multiple-choice and essay questions. An accompanying section gives answers to the multiple-choice questions as well as suggestions for writing the essays. If you have to select a term paper topic, you may choose one from the list of suggestions in this book. This guide also provides you with a reading list, to help you when you start research for a term paper, and a selection of provocative comments by critics, to spark your thinking before you write.

THE AUTHOR AND HIS TIMES

The Glass Menagerie was Tennessee Williams' first successful play. It won the New York Critics' Circle Award as the best play of the 1944-45 Broadway season. Less than three years later, *A Streetcar Named Desire* opened. It, too, captured the Critics' Circle Award and also won the Pulitzer Prize.

With these achievements Tennessee Williams earned fame and lots of money. He was declared one of the best modern playwrights. Had he never written another word, his place on the roster of great artists would still be secure. Usually, he's named with Eugene O'Neill and Arthur Miller as one of the three leading American dramatists of the 20th century.

That's not a bad record for a man of thirty-six. At the time, however, Williams would gladly have given away his success. He liked his plays, but he hated being a celebrity. Success depressed him. As a young man who achieved great success, he suddenly missed the challenges of life. Perhaps you can understand his reaction. Many people who reach glory at an early age realize the emptiness of fame. Autograph seekers depressed him. Strangers who told him "I loved your play" annoyed him. Praise bothered him. He even suspected his friends of false affection. And he felt constant pressure for the rest of his life to write plays as good as *Menagerie* and *Streetcar*.

Williams found relief from the public in a hospital, of all places. He needed an eye operation. When the gauze mask was removed from his face, he viewed his life more clearly, both literally and figuratively. He checked out of his posh New York hotel and escaped to Mexico, where, as a stranger, he could be his former self again.

His former self was Thomas Lanier Williams of Columbus, Mississippi, where he was born in 1911. His maternal grandfather was Columbus' Episcopalian rector. His mother, Edwina, valued refinement and the good manners of Southern gentry. She made sure that Tom and his sister Rose grew up having both. His father, on the other hand, paid little attention to good breeding and culture. He was more fond of a game of poker and a tall glass of whiskey. A traveling salesman, he lived out of suitcases and had little time for his children. Returning from road trips, however, he often criticized his wife for turning young Tom into a sissy.

When Mr. Williams, known as C.C., got an office job with the International Shoe Company, the family settled in St. Louis. Rose and Tom became city children. They played in littered alleys where dogs and cats roamed at night. Or they holed up in a small dark bedroom to play with Rose's prized collection of small glass animals.

Having C.C. around the house strained everyone in the family. C.C. fought with Edwina, disparaged Rose, and sometimes beat Tom. Eventually, he deserted the family altogether, but not until Rose, Tom, and a younger brother, Dakin, had reached adulthood.

Of the three Williams children, Rose had the hardest time growing up. During the early years she and Tom were as close as a sister and brother can be, but in her teens she developed symptoms of insanity. She withdrew into a private mental world. Mrs. Williams could not accept her daughter's illness and tried repeatedly to force friends on her. She enrolled Rose in a secretarial course, but that didn't help Rose's condition either. Diagnosed as a schizophrenic, Rose was put in a mental institution. In 1937 brain surgery turned her into a harmless, childlike woman for the rest of her life.

Tom, who loved Rose dearly, heaped blame for Rose's madness on himself. Not even he understood why. But as he saw it, Rose's terrors started at about the time when he began to feel the irresistible urges of homosexuality. At the time—long before the advent of gay rights—to be a homosexual meant being an outcast. You were scorned and abused, and you were made to feel excruciating guilt. Rose's condition had no bearing on Tom's self-realization, nor did his sexual preferences trigger Rose's breakdown. Yet, the two events became strangely interlocked in Tom's thinking.

In the agonies of his family Williams found the stuff of his plays. He hardly disguised his parents, his sister and himself when he cast them as characters on the stage. Places where he lived became settings, and he adapted plots from life's experiences. He relived the past as he wrote. ("The play is memory," says Tom, the character in *The Glass Menagerie*.) He wrote about what he knew best— himself. Perhaps that's why the plays, although considered dream-like and unreal, can nevertheless, like magic, give you illusion that has the appearance of truth. They often contain an intense passion that could come from only one source, the heart and soul of the playwright.

After high school, Williams went to the University of Missouri to study journalism. His father pulled him out after two years for making low grades and sent him to work at the shoe company. It was a dead-end job, but it gave Tom a chance to do what he loved best—to write. He pushed himself hard to master the art of writing. When the words came slowly, he grew tense. He ate little, smoked constantly and drank only black coffee. After two years his health broke. The doctor ordered him to quit the shoe company.

He enrolled in a play writing course at Washington University in St. Louis. He also started to read widely in world literature. From the Russian Chekhov, he discovered how to make dialogue reveal character. From plays by Ibsen, the Norwegian dramatist, Williams learned the art of creating truth on the stage. Williams owed his fascination with uninhibited sexuality partly to the English writer D. H. Lawrence. He also studied the works of the master Swedish playwright August Strindberg for insights into dramatizing inner psychological strife. Through a friend Williams discovered the American poet Hart Crane, whose lyrical lines and brief tragic life struck a responsive chord in Williams. In all, Williams' prolific reading gave his own writing a boost.

Tom finished his formal schooling at the University of Iowa. When he left there in 1938 he adopted the name "Tennessee." Over the years he offered varying explanations for the new name. It was distinctive. It was a college nickname. It expressed his desire to break away from the crowd, just as his father's pioneering ancestors had done when they helped to settle the state of Tennessee.

With his pen and pad he roamed the United States. Says Tom in *The Glass Menagerie,* "The cities swept about me like dead leaves"—New York, Washington, Los Angeles, Key West, Florida. Also New Orleans, the city of streetcars, including one named "Desire." He wrote stories, poems, even a first play that flopped in Boston. Eventually, he landed a job in California writing screenplays for MGM. But he despised taking others' stories and turning them into movies. He wanted to do originals. While in Hollywood, he wrote a movie script entitled *The Gentleman Caller.* When MGM rejected it, Williams quit his job, transformed the script into a play, and called it *The Glass Menagerie.* The play opened on Broadway in March, 1945, and altered Williams' life. The years of personal struggle to make it big were over.

After moving to Mexico, he turned out a second masterpiece—*A Streetcar Named Desire*—which reached Broadway in December, 1947. In *Streetcar,* as in *The Glass Menagerie,* he shaped the story from his own experience. If you combine Williams' mother, the genteel and prudish Southern lady, with Rose, the fragile sister, you get Blanche. Williams knew firsthand what happens when a brute like Stanley clashes with a refined lady like Blanche. He saw it almost daily in his parents' stormy marriage.

After *Streetcar* Williams turned out plays almost every other season for thirty-five years. According to critics, though, after the 1940's Williams never again reached the heights of *Menagerie* and *Streetcar.* He reused material and seemed continually preoccupied with the same themes and with characters trapped in their own private versions of hell. Although many later plays lacked freshness, others were smash hits and have since joined the ranks of the finest American plays. *Cat on a Hot Tin Roof* won drama prizes in 1955, and *Night of the Iguana* earned honors in 1961.

Because of movies, however, the titles of some of his plays, such as *Suddenly Last Summer* and *The Fugitive Kind* have become familiar, even to people who have never seen a Williams stage play. Some Williams plays (and movies) caused a sensation because they deal with homosexuality and incest, topics that had been more or less off limits on the stage and screen until Williams came along. People flocked to Williams movies to see stars like Elizabeth Taylor, Richard Burton and Paul Newman. In the film of *A Streetcar Named Desire*, Marlon Brando and Vivian Leigh gave magnificent performances as Stanley and Blanche.

All of Williams' plays illustrate a dark vision of life, a vision that grew dimmer as the years went by. During his last years Williams kept writing, but one play after the other failed. To ease his pain, Williams turned to drink and drugs. His eyes needed several operations for cataracts. The new plays received terrible notices, driving him deeper into addiction. He died in a New York hotel room in 1983. Police reports say that pills were found under his body.

Williams left behind an impressive collection of work. His plays continue to move people by their richness, intensity of feeling, and timelessness. He often transformed private experience into public drama. In doing so, he gave us glimpses into a world most of us have never seen before. Yet, the plays make Williams' fears, passions, and joys ours as well. Few artists will ever leave behind a more personal and intense legacy.

The Glass Menagerie

THE PLAY

The Plot

How does a young man with the mind and heart of a poet wind up as a sailor in the merchant marine? Tom Wingfield can tell you. He's done it. Years ago, he ran away from home and joined up.

One reason Tom left home was his mother, Amanda. She drove him to it. How? You'll see the instant you meet her. She nags Tom about his smoking, scolds him about getting up in the morning, and instructs him in the fine art of chewing food. It isn't easy to have a mother like Amanda. Yet Tom put up with her until one tragic night when his patience ran out, and he abandoned his family.

Of course Tom may simply be following in his father's footsteps. Mr. Wingfield deserted his family years ago, leaving Amanda to raise Tom and his sister Laura in a run-down tenement in the St. Louis slums. Amanda is used to better. She repeatedly recites stories of gracious young gentlemen who came to court her on the veranda of her family's plantation. But she married Mr. Wingfield, and ever since, she copes with life by recalling gentle days in the Old South. The details often change, however, and her children sometimes suspect Amanda's stories to be mere fabrication.

Lately, Amanda has begun to notice similarities between Tom and her husband. Tom is bored with life and very restless. Down at the warehouse he ducks into the washroom during slow hours and writes poems. Every night, after a dull day of work, he escapes to the movies—for adventure, he says. Amanda is worried that Tom drinks. She fears that Tom will run away. She gets him to promise that he won't leave, at least not until his sister has a good man to provide for her.

Laura, in fact, is Amanda's gravest problem. A childhood disease has left her partly lame. She is frail and terribly insecure. Although she's older than Tom, she's never held a job. One attempt to send her to a business school ended dismally. She, like Tom, escapes to an unreal world, spending most of her time listening to old records and playing with her collection of glass animals. What the future holds for Laura, Amanda can't even guess.

That's why Amanda hounds Tom to bring home a friend, some eligible young man who will fall for Laura and marry her. Tom agrees, not because he thinks Amanda's scheme will work, but because he has pledged himself to help Amanda before he leaves home. Tom invites Jim O'Connor, an acquaintance from work. Amanda is thrilled, but Laura gets sick with fright.

Jim turns out to be someone Laura knew and admired from a distance back in high school. He charms Amanda and treats Laura kindly. He advises Laura to feel more sure of herself. To be a success you need confidence, he tells her. He shows her how to dance, and gently kisses her. In every respect, Jim seems like Laura's rescuer, the man to save her from a life of dependency and illusions. While dancing, they accidentally break the horn from Laura's prized glass unicorn. Now it looks like an ordinary horse. Symbolically, Jim has released Laura from her dream world.

But Laura's excursion into reality is a short-lived disaster. Jim won't be calling on Laura again. He's already engaged to be married. When Amanda finds out, she accuses Tom of deliberately making a fool of her. In her fury, Amanda refuses to hear Tom's denials. For Tom, this is the last straw. He packs up and leaves. Literally, he escapes.

But he fails to escape completely. As he wanders the earth, searching for some elusive paradise, the memory of his sister haunts him.

You're left with the thought that happiness, like so much else in Tom's life, is an illusion, too.

The Characters

Tom Wingfield

When Tennessee Williams created Tom he pulled a neat trick. He created a character who exists outside *and* inside the play's action at the same time. When you see him standing on the fire escape adjoining the Wingfield apartment, Tom is the narrator. He is outside the action. He is a seasoned merchant sailor who's traveled on both land and sea. He's a good talker, too, the kind you might like to spend an evening with over a few beers. He can be funny, as when he describes his runaway father as a "telephone man who fell in love with long distances."

One actor's reading of Tom's lines can give you the impression that Tom regrets being a wanderer. Another actor can create the sense that Tom looks back with relief, pleased that he broke away, at least from his mother. Regardless of the interpretation you favor, you know that Laura, Tom's sister, has a firm hold on his affections. "Oh, Laura, Laura," he says in the play's final speech, "I tried to leave you behind me, but I am more faithful than I intended to be!" Evidently, memory is a potent force, one that Tom can't escape. Or, looking at Tom's character yet another way, you might conclude that he has stepped beyond the bounds of a brotherly concern for Laura into a more forbidding relationship.

Because the whole play is Tom's memory brought to life on the stage, Tom may be the most important character. However, you could make a case for Amanda's importance as well. Either way, Tom sets the sentimental mood of the play and reveals only what he wants you to know about his family. If Amanda narrated the play, can you imagine how different it would be?

Tom calls himself a poet. He writes poetry at every opportunity. You hear poetic speeches pour from his lips. A co-worker at the warehouse calls him "Shakespeare." Does he deserve the name? Do any of his speeches sound like poetry to you?

In addition, Tom claims a poet's weakness for symbols. In fact, the story bulges with symbols of all kinds, some obvious (the little glass animals signifying Laura), some more obscure (frequent references to rainbows, for example). For a full discussion of symbolism in the play, see the Symbol section of this volume.

You rarely see Tom in a cheerful mood. He complains, groans, sulks, argues, or pokes fun at others, especially at Amanda. He bristles under her constant nagging. He quarrels about inviting home a beau for Laura. Most of all, he is repelled by Amanda's repeated references to her long-ago past. Why do Amanda's stories bother him so? Is his reaction typical of children listening to parents recount tales of their youth?

Tom's resentful manner leads his mother to accuse him of having a "temperament like a Metropolitan [Opera] star." Does Amanda have a point? Is Tom preoccupied with pleasing himself? Or do you sympathize with Tom? Tom's obligations seem to tear him apart. He's caught between responsibilities to his family and to himself. In short, he faces a dilemma that's often part of growing up. Which, in your opinion, ought to take precedence: family responsibility or personal ambition?

To cope with frustration and pain Tom sometimes uses bitter humor. When Amanda accuses him of leading a shameful life, he knows it's futile to argue. So he jokes with his mother about his second identity as "Killer Wingfield" and "*El Diablo*," the prince of the underworld. Or when Amanda is about to start reminiscing about Blue Mountain, he comments ironically to Laura, "I know what's coming."

Humor provides only a little relief, however. That's why he rushes off to the movies whenever he can. Watching someone else's adventures on the movie screen offers Tom another diversion from his own dreary existence. But since he has to come out of the dark theater and face life again, escape to the movies solves no problems. At great cost Tom learns that running away from problems never clears them from your mind. Even when he flees St. Louis, he takes along his memories as mental baggage. He can't escape the past, however hard he tries. Escape, he discovers in the end, is an illusion, too.

What Tom tells you as he stands at the edge of the stage may be more than just the story of one young man's disillusion. You might think of Tom as a representative of a whole generation of young people coming of age just as the world is exploding into war. They have high hopes and rich dreams. But the future they wish for never comes. It is destroyed by forces beyond their control. "The world is lit by lightning," Tom says.

Tom's story, then, may be both personal and generally symbolic of life at a bleak time in our history. You can read it either way.

Amanda Wingfield

In the production notes of *The Glass Menagerie*, Tennessee Williams tells you that Amanda is "a little woman of great but confused vitality clinging frantically to another time and place. . . . There is much to admire in Amanda, and as much to love and pity as there is to laugh at." Do you agree? Do you find her as difficult to bear as Tom does?

In contrast to Tom, who sets the mood in the play, Amanda is a mover, the character who sets the story into motion. Therefore, you might consider her the play's main character. Throughout the play Tom, Laura and Jim respond to Amanda's stimulating and complex personality. Even her husband, who has run from her, showed a distinctive response to Amanda. Tom shares a few tender moments with his mother, but more typically, he's put off by her scolding and nagging. Laura, unlike her brother, usually obeys Amanda's wishes and tries to understand her. Jim, during dinner with the Wingfields, is caught up by Amanda's vibrant cheerfulness.

What are you likely to remember most about Amanda? Is it her irrational and inappropriate belief in the romantic past? Or might it be her pathetic conviction that her children are bound to succeed in life because of their "natural endowments?" She refuses to accept the fact that Tom is a malcontent with a dead-end job. As for Laura, Amanda denies that her daughter has anything wrong with her that a little charm and a typing course won't fix. Even Jim O'Connor, quite an ordinary young man, strikes Amanda as a shining prince destined to rescue and marry Laura. Amanda's wishes for her children sometimes leave her blind to reality.

To understand Amanda you should decide whether she is really as far gone as she often appears. Is she unaware of the truth, or does she simply refuse to accept it? Despite her frequent silliness, she evidently has a practical streak. She thinks seriously about the future. That's why she presses Tom to bring home a friend for Laura.

Obviously, Amanda acts foolish much of the time. But she nevertheless has admirable qualities. Amanda tries hard to be a good mother. After her husband runs off, she does the best she can to provide for her family. Above all, she is strong, stronger than Tom and stronger than her husband. When all her efforts have failed, she sticks by Laura. She emerges tender and noble. And you can depend on her never to give up hope. At the end of the play, with Tom enroute to the seven seas and Laura brokenhearted over Jim, Amanda shows "dignity and tragic beauty." What, in your opinion, is the source of Amanda's transformation? Or might she have had dignity and tragic beauty within her all along?

Laura Wingfield

It's more than coincidental that the play's title refers to the collection of glass animals that belongs to Laura. She is so fragile that she can hardly function in the real world. Not surprisingly, her favorite figure in the menagerie is the unicorn, a creature which Laura calls "freakish," which is precisely the way Laura has felt much of her life. Can you think of other qualities of the unicorn that resemble Laura?

Laura frequently escapes to a private, imaginary world occupied by fragile glass animals. When you consider Laura's personality, can you speculate on why the menagerie is glass rather than some other material?

Of the three Wingfields, Laura stands in the greatest peril, for she lacks both the strength of Amanda and the potential to escape, like Tom. Laura creates the impression that she's forever going to be a misfit. The world is simply too harsh for her. She confesses to Jim how awkward she felt in high school. She wore a brace on her leg and believed that everyone in school noticed her "clumping" around. As people grow older they usually overcome feelings of shyness. Why didn't Laura?

In spite of her fragility, though, Laura is the most serene member of her family. She leaves the worrying to Amanda and Tom. Sometimes she may remind you of a child who creates havoc and doesn't know it. In her innocence, Laura doesn't realize how Tom and Amanda bleed for her.

It's possible to think of Laura as merely a timid, neurotic little girl, totally absorbed in her own troubles. But can you find more substance in her character? Is she sensitive to Amanda and to Tom in any way? Does she contribute to the well being of her family? You may not have to search far to find likeable and sympathetic traits in Laura's personality.

Laura hides in her make-believe world. Only once, during Jim O'Connor's visit, does she venture out of it into the world of reality. Jim has given Laura a bit of self-confidence. He even convinces her to dance with him. During the dance, they bump the table, knocking the glass unicorn to the floor and breaking off its single horn. Do you see the symbolism of this mishap? Laura, for a short time, feels like any other girl who has been swept off her feet by the boy of her dreams. Unfortunately for Laura, though, the time of her life lasts no more than a few minutes.

When Tom leaves home for good, why do thoughts of Laura haunt his memory? Is he plagued by guilt? Does he love her more than a brother should? Does Laura have charms that have gotten under his skin?

Jim O'Connor

Tom tells you in his opening speech that Jim is an emissary from the world of reality. If that is so, reality must be a fairly dull place, for Jim is a nice, but rather ordinary, young man. On the surface, he is well-mannered, hard-working, and responsible. He is a pleasant guest, and he dutifully entertains Laura after dinner. He does all you'd expect him to. Why, then, is Jim so disappointing?

Even Jim himself knows that he's a disappointment, although he puts up a smooth-talking and self-confident front. When you consider his admirable high school record, he should be racing up the ladder of success by now. Instead, he's still in the pack.

Common wisdom, which Jim believes, says that if you work hard, you'll succeed. Jim has worked hard, but he hasn't succeeded. So he takes self-improvement courses in public speaking, thinking that greater "social poise" will help him land the executive position of his dreams. He's also studying radio engineering in order to get in on the ground floor of the new television industry. He seems to be doing all the right things and saying the right things, too, about opportunity and progress in America. But the ideas sound trite, as though Jim is mouthing someone else's words.

Although he's trying hard, you never know if Jim will make it big. Perhaps he will. On the other hand, when you recall that illusion dominates the play, you might suspect that Jim's plans are pure fancy, and that he's placed too much faith in a hollow dream. In the end, he may just plod along like everyone else.

After dinner at the Wingfields Jim is pleased with

himself for winning Laura so easily. His conquest reminds him of his high school days when he held the world in his hands. Laura is good for his ego. He's driven to pursue his dream, even if he has to step on others as he goes. Finally, he dismisses Laura with the news that he's engaged. Dinner at the Wingfields' turns out to be only a brief stop along the way to elusive success.

Should Jim have revealed his engagement earlier in the evening? Was he under any obligation to do so? Or was it all right for him to wait until the end of his visit? If he had told his marriage plans earlier, Laura would have missed a few moments of happiness. Does that fact by itself justify Jim's action? What would you have done under similar circumstances?

Other Elements

SETTING

The whole play is set in the Wingfields' apartment, which faces an alley in the downtown slums of St. Louis. In the stage directions Tennessee Williams draws a vivid picture of the place. It's cramped and dark, almost like a jail cell. You can't tell it apart from the thousands of other apartments occupied by people trapped in drab and joyless lives. No one in the family wants to live there. But poverty forces them to. It shouldn't surprise you that "escape" develops into a major theme in the play.

The drawing on page 18 shows you how the apartment might be arranged for a performance. In addition to the usual rooms, there is an important fire escape off to one side. The characters in

Kitchen

Record Player

Scrim Wall

Photo of Mr. Wingfield

Daybed

Scrim Wall

Dining Room

Table & Chairs

Mirror

Scrim Wall

Lamp

Typewriter

Phone

Scrim (Exterior Wall of Apartment Building)

Living Room

Glass Menagerie

Chair

AUDIENCE

Alley

Fire Escape

Window

Dance Hall

the play sometimes stand on the fire escape. Tom delivers his speeches to the audience from there. The family uses it to go in and out every day. But it's an "escape" only in name because the people living here are "fundamentally enslaved" in their lower middle-class lives.

Across the alley you see the Paradise Dance Hall. Much of the music you hear during the play comes from there. Sometimes the melodies are subtle comments on events taking place in the Wingfield apartment. Almost every detail of the setting in some manner suggests a theme or contributes an idea to the play. Consider, for instance, the name "Paradise Dance Hall." The young people who meet and dance there will soon be going to war. Many will be killed. Could Williams be implying that this two-bit dance hall is as close to paradise as those boys and girls will ever get?

Think also of the smiling photo of Mr. Wingfield prominently displayed on the wall. Isn't it odd that Amanda, who expresses disdain for her husband, keeps it there? Perhaps Amanda preserves the photograph as a souvenir, a remembrance from the past. Or the photo, which hangs in the living room, may also be kept there to serve as a daily reminder to the Wingfields—especially Tom—that escape is possible.

When Tom steps onto the fire escape to introduce you to the play, the 1940's have begun, and World War II is raging. In his story, he takes you back to the 1930's, a decade of hopeless depression.

You might ask why Tennessee Williams wants you to know the world situation during the time of the story. After all, affairs of state don't directly touch Tom and the other characters. Is the play, then, meant to be more than just a drama of family life? Can you find parallels between the events in the apartment and events in the world? Would the play be less poignant if you didn't know about the civil war in Spain, the massive poverty of the Great Depression, and the growth of Nazism? As you think about the play, these are questions worth considering.

THEMES

The following are themes of *The Glass Menagerie*.

1. ILLUSION

We all have illusions. You can hardly live without them. Usually, they are harmless thoughts about, say, last summer's vacation or that very attractive person you just met. Whenever you hold an opinion based on what you think is true, or should be true, rather than what actually is true, that's an illusion. Because illusions sometimes help you deal with painful facts, like good medicine they make you feel better. But when you are *dis*illusioned, the pain returns.

The characters in *The Glass Menagerie* are hooked by their illusions. Without illusion, Amanda would realize the hopelessness of Laura's condition. In fact, it's *because* of her illusions that Amanda keeps her hopes alive for that "always expected something" to rescue Laura from a life of dependency. Initially, Amanda thinks that a good typing course will help Laura pull herself together. And later in the play, Amanda foolishly counts on Jim to be Laura's prince charming. Amanda, of course, also has illusions about herself. Whether she really entertained seventeen gentleman callers one Sunday afternoon is beside the point. What counts is that she believes it. Illusions, you see, can be very powerful.

Tom suffers from illusions, too, by expecting to find adventure in the movies. When he leaves home and joins the merchant navy he anticipates more adventure. Does that fire escape lead to romance and glamor? Study his final speech for an answer. Note that Tom is haunted by reminders of Laura. Is escape, in the end, an illusion, too?

The imaginary world of glass animals provides Laura's refuge from reality. But in her case, illusion may be perilous, for her menagerie serves as a substitute for life. How long can she go on playing with the glass collection before disillusion strikes?

Jim O'Connor, like the other young people Tom tells you about, is also living in an illusion. When success eludes him he places faith in the future. But the future he counts on is an illusion, for there's a terrible war just around the corner that's going to change the world forever.

2. ESCAPE

The theme of illusion is first cousin to the theme of escape in *The Glass Menagerie*, for all the play's characters believe incorrectly that escape from their present situation in life is possible. Tom tries repeatedly to escape from tedium and responsibility. Amanda indulges at times in reveries about her girlhood. The glass menagerie serves as Laura's means of escape from reality, and Jim tries desperately to escape from his dead-end job by taking public speaking and radio courses.

Observe that no character in the play makes a

clean break from his situation. Correction: only Mr. Wingfield escapes—at the expense of his family's happiness, but that took place before the play begins.

A fire escape symbolically points the way out of the Wingfield apartment. But when Laura uses it, she stumbles. When Tom leaves for good he claims to follow in his father's footsteps, but he is pursued by "something." A powerful love? Guilt? He tried to leave Laura behind, but couldn't. His closing speech reveals how securely he is bound to the past.

What conclusion about escape can you draw from the situation in the play? Does the play advise you to make the best of what you've got, because change is impossible? Note Mr. Wingfield's smiling portrait. Does the grin tell you anything?

3. FRAGILITY

Can you think of anyone who embodies the idea of fragility better than Laura? Both physically and psychologically, she is fragile. A childhood disease left her with a slight limp. Under the everyday stresses of life, her composure shatters, and she can't complete her typing course. The thought of receiving a gentleman caller makes her sick. How fitting for Laura to keep a menagerie of delicate glass animals of which the unicorn—the "freakish" one—is her favorite.

The characters in The Glass Menagerie have built their lives on a fragile foundation of illusions. Take away their illusions and which of them would not break?

In 1939, the time of the play, world peace is in a fragile state. The lives of the young lovers who kiss in the alley will soon be shattered by big guns and heavy bombardments.

4. LIGHT

Because *The Glass Menagerie* is a memory play, the setting is dimly lighted. Dim lights keep details from being seen, for details fade from the memory first.

The electric company turns off the Wingfields' power. Then the characters must resort to candles, which soften the illumination and add the aura of romance to Jim's visit with Laura.

Light shining through little glass objects often gives off tiny spots of rainbow color. A rainbow, as you probably know from the old song, is something you chase. And in biblical myth, the rainbow is the symbol of a promise. But when you get close it vanishes. It's an illusion, a false promise, like so much else in the play. Tom recognizes the illusory quality of rainbows. He says the pleasures offered by the Paradise Dance Hall were "like a chandelier [which] flooded the world with brief deceptive rainbows." Notice also that the scarf given as a souvenir by Malvolio the Magician is rainbow-colored. In the end, what is it that keeps Laura embedded in Tom's memory? Shop windows, "filled with pieces of colored glass . . . like bits of shattered rainbow."

Tom associates images of Laura with candlelight. To rid himself of the haunting memories of his sister, he implores Laura to "blow out your candles." At the same time Tom may be urging Laura out of her dimly lit past. Her world of candlelight and little glass animals will no longer do, for "nowadays the world is lit by lightning."

5. FAILURE AND THE MYTH OF SUCCESS

Amanda believes in several common myths about money, success, and working hard. She thinks that money, for example, buys happiness. If she had only married one of those rich gentlemen callers. . . .

Then, too, she admires sophisticated society, the "horsey set" portrayed in the magazine stories she sells.

Success, in her view, comes from hard work and from saving your money for the future. Amanda is convinced that Tom will be successful if he tries hard. Laura will also succeed if she learns to type. Plan for the future, Amanda advises. Make provisions and save money. To Tom's dismay, she calculates how much money he could save if he stopped smoking. With his savings he could enroll in an accounting course at the university.

Jim O'Connor also chases a dream. He tries to sell Tom "a bill of goods" about success, for he's already bought one that says if you work hard, take the right courses, show self-assurance, and believe in the future of capitalism you'll make it big. But Jim has made little progress since high school, and with the war coming on, the path to success is likely to be detoured.

The personal failure of all the characters in the play in some ways parallels the larger social failure of America. The Depression turned millions of American dreams into nightmares. And the only way out was no better. It took a catastrophic war to release the country from poverty and fear.

STYLE

Almost from the outset you know that *The Glass Menagerie* is going to be a poetic play. Your first clue is Tom's playful use of words. Tom announces, "He gives you illusion that has the appearance of truth. I give you truth in the pleasant disguise of illusion." He also uses metaphors ("the middle class of America was matriculating in a school for the blind"), and his language is often alliterative as in "fingers pressed forcibly down on the fiery Braille. . . ." But in case you missed all that, Tom declares outright, "I have a poet's weakness for symbols."

It is not only Tom who endows the play with poetry. Amanda also has a gift for words. She's especially fond of colorful, figurative language. You'll find some in almost all her lengthy speeches, as in her lecture to Laura about the hopelessness of the future (Scene Two): "—stuck away in some little mousetrap of a room . . . like birdlike women without any nest—eating the crust of humility. . . ."

Because Tennessee Williams had his own mother in mind when he created Amanda, he tried to make her sound like a dignified Southern lady. (Her lines ought to be spoken with a Southern drawl.) Nothing tasteless or vulgar passes her lips. She often uses the sort of flowery language you'd expect to hear on a veranda in the Old South: "liquid refreshment" for *drink*, "position" instead of *job*, and "handsome appearance" rather than *good looks*.

In addition, Amanda wants to impose her taste in words on her children. She rejects Tom's books as "filth." Also, because she thinks the word "cripple" is offensive, she won't permit Laura to use it. Of course Amanda may deny the word because she refuses to allow Laura to pity herself.

As you study the play some of the symbols, such as Laura's glass menagerie, will virtually explain themselves. You can't miss the similarity between the delicate glass animals and Laura's fragility. On the other hand, you'll have to dig a little to find symbolic meaning in, say, the breaking of the unicorn. At first Jim is a unique hero. But he turns out to be quite ordinary, after all, just as the broken unicorn resembles an ordinary horse. Similarly, during the evening of Jim's visit Laura emerges briefly from her make-believe world into the world of real people leading ordinary lives.

Symbols come in a variety of forms in *The Glass Menagerie*. You can readily assign symbolic importance to objects (e.g., candles, rainbows, typewriter chart) and to actions (Laura's tripping on the fire escape, Tom's moviegoing). Tom describes Jim O'Connor as a symbolic character who represents deferred hopes for the future. Many of the images projected on the screen suggest deeper meanings, too. Take, for example, "Jolly Roger" (Tom's desire for adventure) and "Annunciation" (the news that Jim is coming to dinner). Perhaps the whole play, acted out behind transparent screens and dimly lit, symbolizes the workings of memory. As you search through the text for symbols you're not likely to come up empty handed. But guard against turning everything into a symbol. You need to support your interpretations with solid evidence from the play.

POINT OF VIEW

Tom is both a character in the play and the play's narrator. At the very beginning and at several points along the way Tom, as narrator, stands on the fire escape outside the Wingfields' apartment and addresses you directly. He tells you about a period of time—about three or four years ago—when he broke away from his mother and sister and became a wanderer. He also sets the scene, establishes the mood, comments on the world situation, and gives you background information.

You know how hard it sometimes is to remember details of events that happened only yesterday? Tom knows, too, that you can't always depend on your memory. So rather than trying to re-create precisely what took place several years ago, he presents the story unrealistically. At dinner, for example, the characters don't use real dishes and utensils. They pretend to be eating. And if the actors are good, the illusion is quite satisfactory.

"Memory," the playwright tells you in his stage directions, "takes a lot of poetic license" because it is "seated predominantly in the heart." Consider Williams' words a fair warning that what you see on stage is only approximately what happened in reality. Every event has been filtered by time and by Tom's feelings. Amanda's nagging is supposed to irritate you, just as it irritates Tom. If at any time you find Laura particularly lovely or especially helpless, consider those impressions to be Tom's, too. In short, Tom is your emotional guide through the play.

You may notice that Tom's vision extends even beyond what he actually saw or experienced. Some scenes include only Laura and Amanda or Jim O'Connor. Since Tom can't know exactly what happened when he wasn't there, he invents dialogue and action and shows you what might have occurred. Is that a flaw in the play?

When people look back to the past, do they recall the good things more readily than the bad? Does Tom? Or do his memories seem more bitter than sweet? Or are his recollections flavored by both? Tom often speaks ironically. Note how he describes Amanda on the phone in Scene Three. Is Tom's humor biting? Or do you find it gentle, touched by nostalgia? Tom calls the play "sentimental," which suggests Tennessee Williams' intentions.

FORM AND STRUCTURE

The play has seven scenes. The first four take place over a few days' time during the winter season. The remaining scenes occur on two successive evenings during the following spring. Since the play contains no formal "acts," a director can prescribe an intermission at any time. How would you divide the play if you were directing a performance? In formulating your answer take into account the passage of time, climactic moments in the play, and the development of the characters. Why do you suppose Williams chose not to tell you where to break the action?

Williams attempted to unify the several episodes by devising a series of projected images and words on a screen, but most directors don't bother using the technique. The story, they feel, can stand unaided, despite repeated jumps between present and past.

Tom, the narrator, exists in the present. He talks directly to the audience at the start of the play, at the openings of Scenes Three and Six, and again at the end. Also, he steps briefly into the narrator's shoes part way through Scene Five.

The rest of the time Tom is a character in the play. Even at those times, however, your focus is shifted to the past. Amanda, for example, frequently recalls her life as a young girl, and Laura and Jim refer to their high school days, which ended six years before.

Because the play comes from Tom's memory, time loses its usual sequence and structure in *The Glass Menagerie*. In your memory, thoughts can bounce at will between the recent and distant past. That may explain the play's flow of events. During most of the play Tom's memory is fastened to the period just before he leaves home. Each episode in the play helps to explain why in the end Tom had no choice but to escape. If you examine his closing speech, however, you'll see whether or not he truly escaped.

The Play
SCENE ONE

Tennessee Williams gives you a lengthy set of stage directions at the start. He wants you to see the run-down tenement where the Wingfield family lives, and he wants to create a mood that combines dinginess, desperation and depression. After you are familiar with the play, return to the opening scene and reexamine Williams' choice of details: the fire escape, the alley, the blown-up photo of smiling Mr. Wingfield, and the typewriter keyboard chart. All, you will see, play important roles somewhere in *The Glass Menagerie*.

When Tom steps out on the fire escape to talk to the audience, he tells you the social background of the play (the 1930's). He introduces himself and the play's other characters, including his father. Although Mr. Wingfield shows up only in his photograph, he's an influential character in the play. Later on you'll see why.

By the end of Tom's opening speech you know a great deal about him. From his appearance you know he is a merchant sailor. You know, too, that he has a way with words and a "poet's weakness for symbols." His first words—"Yes, I have tricks in my pocket"—alert you to his playful disposition. He's going to trick you by giving you truth in the guise of illusion. That is, he's going to tell you a true story but make it seem unreal. Illusions, you'll soon see, pile up one after the other as the play proceeds.

NOTE: On illusion   The very nature of theater depends on illusion. When you watch a play you make believe that the actors on stage *are* the characters they portray. The better the acting, the more easily you accept the illusion. Here Tom forewarns you that the play is unreal. The characters, setting, props, effects, and so on are not meant to be real but rather to serve as metaphors and symbols of reality.

While illusion is part of any play, it is particularly vital in this one. Illusion, in fact, is a major theme. The characters survive because their illusions protect them from the painful facts of their lives. As you continue, keep in mind that illusions can prove to be self-destructive as well as helpful.

Do the Wingfields' illusions create damage, or are they merely harmless aspects of their personalities?

The very first "trick" Tom has in store is a quick change in identity. In a moment, he leaves his role as narrator and as a younger man walks into the Wingfield dining room to join his mother Amanda and sister Laura at supper.

NOTE: Tom shifts between his role as narrator and his role as a character several times during the play. As narrator Tom moves the story from one episode to the next, informs you about himself and his family, and describes the social and political context of the play. Try to compare Tom's personality in his two roles. The narration takes place years after the story's events occurred. Do you notice differences between the two Toms? Which do you prefer? Think of what might have happened to him between the time he left his family and the time he comes back to tell his story.

Tom wishes he hadn't sat down, for no sooner does he start to eat than Amanda begins to lecture him on the need to chew his food properly. If you've ever been scolded about your table manners, you know how Tom feels. His mother gives advice kindly, but Tom can't stand it. He bolts from the table and reaches for a cigarette. But Amanda doesn't like Tom's smoking any more than his chewing.

NOTE: On staging the play   Tom's cigarette is probably imaginary, just like the table knives and forks. Remember, the play is not supposed to be realistic. Still another unrealistic feature is the use of legends and images projected on a screen. The legend which preceded this dinner scene reads "Ou sont les neiges," a phrase from an old French poem which asks, "Where are the snows of yesteryear?" The answer, of course, is "gone," just as the past is always gone. This legend lends an element of nostalgia to your feelings for Amanda. Throughout the play you will find other phrases and pictures. What, if anything, do they add to the play? Some critics have said they detract from the drama. Do you agree?

Laura offers to bring in the dessert. Is she being helpful or does she simply want to avoid listening to her mother nag Tom? Either way, Amanda stops Laura and says she'll play the "darky," a word that gives you a clue to Amanda's origins. She's from the South.

From the kitchen, Amanda begins to tell her children about the gentlemen callers she had as a girl in Blue Mountain. You can tell from Tom and Laura's reaction that they've heard the story before. Laura listens politely. Tom, on the other hand, is skeptical and impatient. Their reactions are important clues to their personalities and to the roles they play in the family. Because the facts of the tale change from time to time, Tom teases Amanda and utters sarcastic comments. He doesn't believe a word she says.

Does Amanda herself believe the story she's fond of telling? Does she really think that seventeen wealthy young admirers came to call on her one Sunday afternoon in Blue Mountain? You'll see later in the play that Amanda often twists truths. Does that mean she's a liar? She doesn't deceive anyone, and she's not out to harm anyone with her inventions. In fact, her intent is quite admirable, for she wants to help Laura find romance in her life. Many think that she deserves a pat on the back for her efforts. Tom, however, rejects Amanda's fantasy.

SCENE TWO

Alone in the apartment, Laura washes and polishes her glass collection. At the sound of her mother's footsteps outside, Laura hurriedly stows her menagerie and pretends to study the typing chart on the wall. Why doesn't she want to be caught caring for her glass animals? At the instant of Amanda's entrance, Laura starts to explain that she was just studying the chart. But as though she sees right through the pretense, Amanda says, "Deception? Deception?" But it's another deception that Amanda has in mind.

She acts brokenhearted, weeping and lamenting as though a terrible tragedy has occurred. She makes the most of this opportunity to play the role of betrayed mother. She is so melodramatic that you can't take her too seriously. She even yanks the typing chart from the wall and tears it into pieces. Meanwhile, Laura behaves as though she can't possibly imagine what has kindled Amanda's dismay. Laura may well suspect the origin of the trouble, however. For weeks she's been skipping her typing classes at Rubicam's Business College.

Sure enough, Amanda has found out. Typing seems like a fairly harmless course, but not for one as fragile as Laura. The pressure made her so sick that she threw up at the school. Then, instead of telling her mother, she has wandered the city each day until it was time to come home. For Laura it was easier to visit the zoo or the park than to reveal the truth and see that "awful suffering look" of disappointment on her mother's face. Does Laura's story sound plausible? While it explains her truancy, does it excuse her deception?

NOTE: On themes   Have you noticed that two interrelated themes—deception and illusion—have just appeared? They will show up repeatedly in numerous variations throughout the play. You should have no trouble spotting them.

In this scene both Amanda and Laura have practiced deception, pretending to be what they are not: Laura posed as a student of typing, and Amanda as a mother crushed by her daughter's betrayal. True, Amanda is wounded by Laura, but not to the extent she claims. Any time Amanda meets hard unpleasant facts, she's likely to be hurt. Perhaps that's why she often makes up illusions. Pretending keeps painful truths at arm's length.

For now, Amanda is caught in the illusion that Laura's problems will be solved by a typing course. Would you agree that learning to type seems like an effective way to solve Laura's problems? Laura herself doesn't seem to think so. She acts as though it's perfectly okay to play with her menagerie instead of working. She chooses to walk in the park instead of owning up to failure. When Laura says "I couldn't face it," she analyzes her condition accurately. She truly cannot face reality. And when Amanda discovers the truth about Laura, she has the urge to "find a hole in the ground and hide myself in it forever!"

Laura apparently fails to share her mother's concern about the future. She never talks about it, and despite Amanda's warnings, she does nothing to prepare for it. Laura seems almost like a small child in that respect.

Compared to Laura, Amanda is almost a realist. Experience has taught her that unless you earn a living you will inevitably depend on others all your life, eating the "crust of humility." Amanda asks Laura, "Is that the future we've mapped out for ourselves?"

The only choice left, of course, is marriage. Perhaps Amanda has considered it and discarded the notion for Laura. Remember that her own marriage turned out badly. What would Laura do if she, like Amanda, ended up with a runaway husband? Also, as far as we know, Laura has never had a date.

Regardless, Amanda's spirits are revived by the thought of Laura's marriage. Since Laura isn't cut out for a business career, she'll have to marry a nice young man. Laura objects: "I'm—crippled!" But Amanda won't hear it. She doesn't even want Laura to say the word.

NOTE: Does Laura have a point? Is she truly "crippled"? She limps just slightly. Would you say that she is more psychologically than physically crippled? What do you know about her thus far to suggest that she'll always have a hard time functioning in the world?

Amanda cringes at the word "crippled." She told Laura never to use the word. Perhaps Amanda believes in the power of words. That is, if you tell a lie often enough, after a while you begin to believe it. In what respects does this saying seem to be valid in *The Glass Menagerie?*

SCENE THREE

Tom returns as narrator to tell you about Amanda's obsession: finding a nice young man to marry Laura. If you have ever known someone with a one-track mind you can appreciate what Amanda must have been like at the time. She even took a part-time job selling magazine subscriptions by telephone to earn extra money for re-doing both Laura and the apartment. Amanda is a woman of action as well as words.

While Tom doesn't object to his mother's frantic activities, he doesn't support them either. Rather, he thinks they are amusing. At least he seems to poke gentle fun at Amanda's efforts. But do you note an ache in Tom's recollection of Amanda on the telephone with Ida Scott? He remembers how pathetically Amanda tried to ingratiate herself with a customer who obviously didn't care. Rather than admit to his pain, Tom recalls the situation with bitter humor. Like many people who demonstrate a talent for laughter when their emotions are stirred, Tom may laugh to keep from crying. What does

Tom's attitude reveal about his deepest feelings toward his mother?

NOTE: As you continue with the play you'll have numerous chances to laugh at comical lines (mostly Tom's) and situations. Some of the humor may be pure, unadulterated fun. But some of it may strike you as humorous only until you realize that the words or actions grow out of the characters' desperation. Would Amanda, for instance, find humor in Tom's rendition of her quest to find Laura a husband?

When Tom steps back into his role in the play, you find him embroiled in a shouting match with his mother. Evidently, she has interrupted him at his writing and has criticized the books he reads. "I won't allow such filth brought into my house!" screams Amanda. Tom won't permit Amanda to claim their apartment as "my house," for his salary pays the rent. Consider Tom's reasoning. Does the fact that he is the family breadwinner give him the right to disregard his mother's wishes?

The fury between mother and son intensifies. Tom is about to curse at his mother and rush out the door. Laura desperately calls out: "Tom!" At the sound of her voice, the shouting diminishes. Tom, now in control of his passion, talks intensely to Amanda about how he hates the life he leads.

NOTE: On Laura Do you find yourself taking sides in the fight between Amanda and Tom? You're not given much choice when the antagonists are a bossy, narrow-minded woman and her selfish, irresponsible son. Since Tom and Amanda will fight to a draw anyway, pay attention to Laura's role in the conflict. Isn't she, after all, the reason that Tom and Amanda fight? If there were no Laura, Tom would probably have moved out of the house long ago, and Amanda would have no one to worry about but herself. As in all families, each member has a particular function. In the Wingfield household, Laura serves as peacemaker. You'll see her step between Tom and Amanda several more times in the play.

Tom's catalog of grievances includes a miserable job at the Continental Shoemakers warehouse. He also hates living in this wretched little apartment where he has a nagging mother, no privacy, and nothing to call his own. He feels like a slave to his job and family. Every morning when Amanda's piercing "Rise and shine!" awakens him, he'd prefer to be dead. No, he's not selfish, Tom replies to Amanda's accusation. If he were, he'd be like his father—gone!

Does Amanda lack compassion for her own son? It may seem so at times. Perhaps fear of the future and anxiety for Laura blind her to Tom's problems. All she can think of is that Tom's erratic and irresponsible behavior jeopardizes her security as well as Laura's. Since both she and Laura depend on Tom for life's necessities, does she have a good reason to be apprehensive? How would you feel about depending on Tom for your livelihood?

As Tom starts to leave again, Amanda grabs at him. "Where are you going?"

"I'm going to the *movies!*" he replies brutally.

She calls him a liar, an accusation which launches him into a semi-tragic, semi-comic list of his nightly sins. Although you can find humor in Tom's speech, you may also be struck by the bitterness of his words. Although his speech is one of the funniest moments in the play, its tone is bitter and sarcastic. Tom concludes by calling Amanda an "ugly— babbling old—*witch. . . .*"

As he rushes from the apartment, his arm gets caught in the sleeve of his bulky coat. Impatiently, he hurls the coat away. It strikes the shelf holding Laura's menagerie, shattering the glass animals. Laura is stunned. When you consider how highly Laura values her menagerie, its wreckage probably marks a turning point in her life. But how sharply she might change remains to be seen. Do you think she has the capacity to change very much?

NOTE: You have seen that all the characters feel trapped by the circumstances of their lives. Since people naturally seek freedom, each has figured out a way to escape, at least temporarily: Amanda uses her illusions, Laura retires to her glass collection, Tom goes to the movies. How well each of these escape mechanisms works becomes clear in the next few scenes. Pay particular heed to Laura. See if the breaking of the glass menagerie sets her free from her illusory world. On the other hand, the damage to the glass could have the reverse effect. That is, it could shatter her inner peace.

Deeply hurt, Amanda calls after Tom, "I won't speak to you—until you apologize."

SCENE FOUR

Slightly drunk, Tom returns to the apartment at five in the morning. Laura opens the door for him. Last night, Tom explains, he went to the movie theater. The stage show featured Malvolio the Magician. (In those days, when you went to the movies, you were offered a full range of entertainment. Movies were often accompanied by live performances.) Malvolio performed tricks of illusion that had the appearance of truth: turning water to wine, then to beer, then to whiskey. But the best trick was Malvolio's escape from a nailed up coffin. Tom says bitterly, "There is a trick that would come in handy for me—get me out of this two-by-four situation."

NOTE: Tom's references to magic and illusions should call to mind the opening of Scene One. You have already observed several examples of deception and illusion in the characters' actions. Stay alert for more in the scenes ahead.

Tom's allusion to his trap—his "two-by-four situation"—reveals that escape is never far from his thoughts. Would it have startled you to learn that Tom had taken permanent leave from home last night after his blow-up with Amanda? He had a tailor-made opportunity to go, but here he is, back again. Why did he come back? What might it take to drive him off for good?

After you hear the six o'clock church bells, Amanda starts her day. Although she's still angry about last night, she unleashes a few "rise and shines" in Tom's direction, but she won't talk to her son. Laura, the peacemaker, tries without luck to get Tom to apologize to Amanda. What do you suppose prevents him from making up?

Soon Amanda sends Laura on an errand to the deli. Laura objects, however. She is afraid to face the scowling deli man when she asks for credit. But she goes, and then slips on the fire escape on her way out.

NOTE: On symbolism It may seem like a trivial incident, but Laura's stumble shouldn't be ignored. Why did the playwright have her stumble on the fire escape? Symbolically, it could suggest the perils of entering the real world.

Some readers object to the search for symbolic meaning in every action or word. Be assured, however, that symbolism in *The Glass Menagerie* is not accidental. Tennessee Williams stated at the outset that the play is full of symbols, but ultimately you're the one who must decide whether to take his statement at face value. You needn't seek symbols in every line of dialogue and each piece of stage business. But if you uncover symbolic treasures as you continue, studying the play may be that much richer an experience for you.

In this scene thus far you might consider the potential symbolism in Tom's rainbow-colored scarf, and the illumination of Mr. Wingfield's photograph. You'll soon be hearing the strains of "Ave Maria," perhaps reminding you that Amanda re-

sembles a suffering madonna when she is deeply
disappointed by her children.

As soon as Tom apologizes, you see the gradual
return of the old Amanda. First she bemoans her
fate and then plays the role of a hurt and troubled
mother: "My devotion has made me a witch and
so I make myself hateful to my children." What
can Tom possibly say in reply, especially after he
has just apologized?

Amanda doesn't give up easily. She wants to
discuss Tom's drinking and moviegoing again,
hoping that Tom will see the connection between
his habits and his sister's future. Tom explains that
because he's restless for adventure, he goes to the
movies. Amanda asserts that most men find adventure in their careers. Of all people, though,
Amanda knows how comforting a short flight into
illusion can be. So she accepts, somewhat reluc-
tantly, Tom's reasons for his nightly escape. Instead of trying futilely to restrain him, Amanda
makes a deal with him. She will not hold him back
if, in return, he provides a man for Laura.

Tom has been manipulated by Amanda, but he
doesn't seem to mind. He probably views the deal
as a small price to pay for freedom. As he goes off
to work, he agrees to bring home a friend from the
warehouse.

SCENE FIVE

Winter has surrendered to spring. The legend
projected on the screen reads "Annunciation,"

suggesting that in this scene an announcement of some note will be made.

NOTE: The "Annunciation" refers to the biblical account of the angel Gabriel's announcement to the Virgin Mary that she was to bear the son of God. The annunciation in this scene may not seem quite as momentous as the original, but to Amanda it is almost as important, as you will see. Also, the feast of the Annunciation is celebrated on March 25, so the legend on the screen helps to note the arrival of spring.

The months have not altered Amanda. She still badgers Tom and laments his lack of ambition. She's still hoping that Tom will settle down, and find contentment as a CPA. Tired of the nagging, Tom retreats to the fire escape, where, as narrator again, he addresses the audience.

He observes life outside the Wingfield apartment. Every evening, young couples used to come to the Paradise Dance Hall to while away hours dancing or kissing in the adjacent alley. That, Tom says, was their form of escape from dull, dreary lives.

Little did these young people know that change was approaching in the form of war. Many of them would be killed fighting the Nazis. But in their innocence, they danced to the music of "The World is Waiting for the Sunrise." As Tom comments, the wait was really for "bombardments."

NOTE: Tom names people and places associated with the coming of World War II. Berchtesgaden = Hitler's mountain headquarters. Chamberlain = British prime minister blamed for failing to stop Hitier's march across Europe. Guernica = a Spanish town destroyed by the fascists in 1937 and which became a symbol for atrocities against innocent people. Pablo Picasso's "Guernica" painting, depicting the horrors of war, is world famous.

On this warm spring evening Amanda joins Tom on the fire escape. While talking with Tom, she sounds much like a young girl flirting with a gentleman caller on the plantation porch. Tom uses the opportunity to give Amanda the news she's been wanting to hear for many months. He has invited a young man, Jim O'Connor, to dinner—tomorrow!

Amanda is ecstatic, of course, but also very businesslike, thinking of what has to be done to prepare for the guest. Her mind races through the list of chores: do the laundry, polish the silver, put up fresh curtains, plan the menu. She quizzes Tom about Jim's job, background, and looks. She wants to know especially if he drinks. Jim would not be right for Laura if he were a drinking man. Although she's just heard of the invitation, Amanda speaks of Jim as Laura's future husband, as a man with family responsibilities. Amanda has probably imagined this moment so often, has anticipated every detail of the courtship, that the news merely triggers the plan into action.

Tom tries to yank Amanda back to reality. He

hasn't told Jim about Laura's existence. The invitation was casual, not couched in terms of "don't you want to meet my sister?" Furthermore, Tom reminds Amanda, Laura is not one to make an instant good impression. She's peculiar, living "in a world of her own—a world of little glass ornaments . . . She plays old phonograph records and—that's about all."

Tom's accurate description of Laura troubles Amanda. But it's only a temporary setback. She has too much invested in her illusion to be waylaid by the truth.

SCENE SIX

You're soon to meet Jim O'Connor, the man designated by Amanda to rescue Laura from a life of dependency. Early in his narration, Tom called Jim a symbolic figure—"the long-delayed but always expected something that we live for." At the start of this scene Tom tells you about the real Jim O'Connor:

Tom recalls that Jim was the most revered student at Soldan High School—popular, talented, athletic—the kind everyone envies. You suspect, too, that Jim is the high school hero Laura liked years ago. But the real world failed to treat Jim as kindly as the world of school. Six years after graduation, he holds only a modest job at the Continental Shoemakers warehouse. Because Tom remembered the days of Jim's triumphs, Jim valued Tom's friendship. He also nicknamed Tom "Shakespeare" for his habit of writing poetry in the warehouse bathroom during slow hours.

Jim's arrival approaches. Amanda has brightened

up the apartment overnight. Laura wears a new dress. The stage directions say that a "fragile, unearthly prettiness has come out in Laura: she is like a piece of translucent glass touched by light, given a momentary radiance, not actual, not lasting." Do you find the last few phrases of that description ominous? Is Laura's prettiness an illusion?

Amanda intends to snare the unsuspecting Mr. O'Connor. The final touch is her own "spectacular appearance." She dons the same party dress that she wore as a girl—the one she wore the day she met her future husband. The garment is totally out of place in a St. Louis tenement, but to Amanda, for the time being, the apartment could just as well be a mansion in Mississippi on the night of the Governor's Ball. Can there be any doubt that Amanda has attempted to re-create a piece of her own youth? If Laura can't win Mr. O'Connor with her lovely fragility, Amanda intends to overwhelm him with charm.

Amanda has kept Jim's name from Laura until now, just a few minutes before her prospective beau is due to arrive. Another little deception, Amanda? Laura is horrified by the revelation. She's overcome with fright and claims to feel sick. She refuses to open the door when the knock comes. Instead, she darts to the record player, her safe haven. But Amanda forces her to let Jim in.

Jim acknowledges Laura, but hardly notices her. He's too involved in telling Tom about a public speaking course he's taking. Jim is also intent on advising Tom to shape up at the warehouse. The boss disapproves of Tom's work and has talked about firing him.

The warning doesn't trouble Tom. Rather, he

almost welcomes it because he knows that he has completed his side of the bargain with Amanda. He tells Jim that he's ready to quit the job anyway. He's even tired of the vicarious thrills he gets in the movies. He wants firsthand excitement now. Tom shows Jim a Union of Merchant Seamen card, which he bought with money that he should have used to pay the light bill. Jim, however, dismisses Tom's revelations as hot air. Could it be that Jim doesn't believe his friend, or that he doesn't understand him?

Presently Amanda, oozing charm, joins the two young men. Her appearance shocks Tom. Even Jim is taken aback slightly. Amanda must think that talking nonstop is the best way to impress Jim. She plunges ahead at full throttle, skipping from topic to topic at random. This is Amanda in her prime, entertaining a flock of gentleman callers in Blue Mountain.

Tom is embarrassed, but Jim, after his initial shock, is won over. He nods and smiles at Amanda's monologue, and during the remainder of the scene says literally only one single word.

Meanwhile Laura remains terror stricken in the kitchen. Her illness is not feigned. Fear has brought on a fever. Amanda explains to Jim that Laura became ill standing over a hot stove. Tom helps Laura into the living room to lie down.

SCENE SEVEN

Although Laura lies huddled on the couch all through dinner, Amanda remains cheerful. She's so high spirited that you'd think that Jim was invited to dinner for her and not for Laura.

No sooner does the scene start than the lights go out. Tom, you've heard, has not paid the light bill, and the electric company has chosen this moment to cut off the power. Can you imagine what Amanda might say about Tom's failure to pay the bill if Jim weren't present?

NOTE: On "light" You have seen numerous references to lights of all kinds throughout the play: moon, lightbulbs, match flame, candlelight, torch, lightning. If moonlight conventionally symbolizes romance, what could lightning represent? Could it be the harsh light of reality? When Tom remarks that "nowadays the world is lit by lightning" he seems to be referring to war. Since a courtship of sorts dominates this scene, you'll see many lights usually associated with romance: candles, moonlight, and so forth. The abrupt loss of electricity, while reminding you that you can't ignore the reality of paying your bills, also provides a convenient reason for using candles to illuminate this "love" scene between Jim and Laura. At the same time, though, keep in mind that the whole play is dimly lit to represent memory.

Amanda manages to remain charming despite the stress she must feel. But even as she banters with Jim, you'll hear hints of seriousness. In a few sentences of apparently light conversation, she mentions the "mysterious universe," the "high price for negligence," and "everlasting darkness." Perhaps these phrases have been included to prepare you for things to come in the play, although you should guard against reading something too ominous into the words.

Finally, Amanda sends Jim into the living room to keep Laura company. To light his way, she gives him an old candelabrum, a relic from the burned-down Church of the Heavenly Rest.

NOTE: On Christian references Are you tempted to seek a symbolic meaning in the church candelabrum? This isn't the first reference to religion in the play, but it comes at a crucial moment. Amanda may view Jim as a "savior" of sorts as he goes to talk to Laura. Could that be the reason she equips him with a holy object? Jim as a Christ figure may be hard for you to accept. Nevertheless, he has been summoned to save Laura. And don't ignore the fact that earlier in the play Amanda plans fish for dinner because Jim is Irish Catholic. Fish, you may know, is a traditional symbol for Christ.

We're about to find out if Amanda's carefully laid plan—or would you prefer to call it a trap?—will work as she hopes. Jim sits down with Laura and talks with her warmly. Frightened and breathless as usual, Laura listens.

Jim dominates the conversation. He's friendly and self assured. Maybe he's practicing what he learned in his courses on how to be successful. His monologue may remind you of Amanda's behavior earlier in the evening. Is he trying to win Laura's admiration as he was won over by Amanda?

Jim obviously likes to talk about himself. Laura is just the opposite. As soon as Jim swings the topic of conversation to Laura's shyness, notice how nimbly Laura tosses the ball back to Jim.

Laura raises the subject of Jim's singing. It's her way of reminding him that they've met before. As they talk, memories of high school come flooding back. Jim remembers that he called Laura "Blue Roses," a name that rhymes with pleurosis, an ailment that kept Laura out of school for a time. The name fits somehow, even six years later, because a blue rose, like Laura, is "different," set apart from others. If you ever see a blue rose, you can bet it's one of a kind.

Laura steers the conversation to Jim's triumphant high school career. When she hands him their high school yearbook (notice its name: *The Torch!*), Jim accepts it "reverently." To Jim, the book is a precious record of his past glory.

Although he delights in recalling the past, Jim keeps his eye on the present. (Remember, Tom labelled Jim "an emissary from the world of reality.") He confesses to Laura that he hasn't yet accomplished all that he once hoped to. Jim's willingness to talk openly emboldens Laura. She asks about Jim's high school sweetheart. The news that he dropped her long ago sends Laura's insides into a tumult. Instinctively, she reaches for her glass menagerie, her haven in times of stress.

Laura wouldn't think of Jim as her "savior" in the religious sense. Yet, he shows the zeal of a missionary in his effort to redeem Laura from life-long feelings of inferiority. Notice his long, sermon-like speeches about the proper way to lead one's life. Christ taught many moral lessons through example. In his preaching, Jim cites his own actions to illustrate self-confidence.

Will Jim actually rescue Laura from misery? If you think so, you're seeing Jim through rose-colored glasses, the way Amanda and Laura do. On the other hand, if Jim strikes you as just an ordinary fellow out for a pleasant evening, you're probably more realistic about him. Look closely at his behavior. Does he truly intend to change Laura? Or does he brag a bit only to boost his own ego?

His advice to Laura could just as well be delivered to himself. It heightens still more his desire to keep striving for success. He's even moved to sing the praises of American democracy.

NOTE: Jim's vision of American democracy is cloudy. It's based on his naive belief that a young person with the right connections and a few night school courses in executive behavior will zoom to the top of the corporate ladder. But how many young people achieve success that way? Jim's plan sounds like an obsolete success myth—that is, an illusion. In addition, Jim ignores the approach of World War II, a real event which postponed or upset virtually every American's plans for the future.

Jim takes a polite interest in Laura's glass collection. Observe how respectfully Jim accepts Laura's fantasy about her unicorn. A less sensitive person might ridicule Laura's notion that the unicorn "loves the light," but not Jim. He's more appreciative than she could wish.

Then he asks Laura to dance. You have to admire him, for who would have thought that anyone could ever get Laura to dance? While dancing they bump the table. The unicorn falls to the floor. Its horn has broken off. Now it's like all the other horses.

NOTE: The symbolism of the unicorn's breakage is as transparent as the glass itself. But that doesn't make it any less poignant or effective. Without its horn, the unicorn is no longer unique. During the evening Laura has broken out of her world of unreality. She, too, has become less "freakish." It's a significant moment in the play.

Jim blames himself for the mishap, but Laura seems not to mind at all. How much Laura has changed! Recall that earlier in the play she had been distraught when Tom knocked the menagerie shelf to the floor. Jim is struck by Laura's graceful good humor as well as by her uniqueness. Suddenly, he's overcome by emotions he can't control. He is tongue tied. He can't think of anything better to do than kiss Laura on the lips.

Jim immediately realizes his mistake. He shouldn't have led her on. Gently, he breaks the news to Laura that he won't be calling again because he's engaged to Betty. Laura is speechless with shock. As Tennessee Williams writes, *"The holy candles on the altar of Laura's face have been snuffed out."* Jim asks Laura to speak, but she can't. Instead, she gives him the broken glass unicorn as a souvenir. A souvenir of what? Of a happy evening? Maybe a token of appreciation for his attempt to help her overcome her problem? Or does she intend to make him feel guilty?

Do you blame Jim for withholding the information about his engagement? Was it wrong for Jim to lead Laura on under false pretenses? Or is he perfectly justified in doing so because he had been invited to dinner only for the purpose of meeting Laura? You might sympathize with him for being a victim of his own conflicting emotions. Perhaps he would like to love Laura, but he feels compelled to hold back because she doesn't fit the mold of a business executive's wife.

Amanda chooses this moment to serve lemonade. As bubbly as before, she encounters a tense and somber situation in the living room. Her gaiety makes the news of Jim's engagement all the more shocking. In a moment, Jim is out the door. Not only has Jim failed to be Laura's knight in shining armor, but he hasn't even been an eligible candidate.

While the evening may not have been a disaster for Laura, it has been for Amanda. She casts about for someone to blame. She won't blame herself, of course, although you might argue that she should have known the risks of investing so much in one evening. Tom, therefore, has to be responsible. Amanda's temper rises. She accuses Tom of deliberate deception, of living in a dream world and manufacturing illusions. Do you see that Amanda could just as easily be talking about herself? In this instance there may be truth in the old idea that we dislike in others what we dislike about ourselves.

Tom refuses to take the blame. It was an innocent mistake, he claims, but Amanda refuses to accept such an excuse. Tom knows his mother well enough to realize he has no hope of dissuading her, so he immediately sets off for the movies. But, as you'll see, he goes much farther. He has fulfilled his obligation at home and can do no more. As he leaves, Amanda shouts after him, "Go to the moon—you selfish dreamer!"

Do you share Amanda's judgment that Tom is a selfish dreamer? You may also appreciate Tom's desperation and his need to do what every young person must do at some point in life: break from home and find one's own identity and place in the world.

NOTE: Tom leaves the apartment in a rage, but he doesn't leave St. Louis until he is fired from his job. If you could look into Tom's head you might find considerable confusion. He wants to leave home, but it's difficult to do so. He also may realize that he could fail to find his dream out in the world. To guard against assuming total responsibility for possible failure, he waits until he is fired. As a result, he can blame his boss instead of himself in case things turn out badly. Tom, like his mother, needs a scapegoat.

Tom's closing speech reviews his wanderings since he left St. Louis. Does he believe that he made the right choice to follow his father's footsteps? Did he find the adventure he sought in the merchant navy? Tom declares that "cities swept about me like dead leaves . . . torn from the branches." Does the statement suggest that world travel suited him?

Why did Tom apparently fail to find the romance he craved? Has life so embittered him that he can't ever be saved from self-pity and sullenness? Or is he guilt ridden over deserting his mother and sister? Still another possibility is that Tom was doomed to chase rainbows. Adventure, romance, excitement—that's what you see in the movies. To pursue them in real life amounts to self-deception, for they are often as elusive as illusions.

Tom can't shake loose his memories of the past. Images of Laura haunt him. His emotional ties to the past may stretch, but they never break. Do you think we are all held captive by our past or is Tom a special case? In the last moment of the play Laura blows out her candles, casting the stage into total darkness. Williams has devised a dramatic ending to the play, but the action also suggests that Tom has finally rid himself of Laura's memory. Why he should suddenly be able to do so, however, is not totally clear. Perhaps the war, symbolized by lightning, has changed everything, including the way men think.

A STEP BEYOND

Test and Answers
TEST

1. Amanda frequently talks about her husband _____
   because she
   A. still loves him in spite of the fact that
      he deserted her
   B. fears that Tom will turn out to be like
      him
   C. wants her children to know their
      family heritage

2. The setting of *The Glass Menagerie* is _____
   unrealistic because
   I. it exists only in Tom's imagination
   II. it is intended to be symbolic
   III. Tom's memory of the details has
      faded
   A. I, II and III   B. I and III only
   C. II and III only

3. Amanda recalls the gentlemen callers of the _____
   past whenever
   A. the present becomes too painful to
      bear
   B. she wants to impress others with her
      social background
   C. Tom insults her

4. Laura usually listens to her mother's stories _____
   of Blue Mountain because she

   A. enjoys hearing them
   B. wants Amanda to enjoy recalling her
      girlhood
   C. expects to learn how to be popular

5. Tom goes to the movies to   _____
    I. get away from Amanda
    II. find adventure
   III. compensate for the boredom of his
       life
   A. I, II and III   B. I and II only
   C. II and III only

6. Amanda and Tom get into an argument over   _____
   A. Tom's reading habits   B. money
   C. Tom's indifference to Laura

7. Tom chooses to invite Jim O'Connor to meet   _____
   Laura because
   A. Jim and Laura knew each other in
      high school
   B. he can't think of anyone else
   C. he owes Jim a favor

8. The Paradise Dance Hall contributes to the   _____
   play as a
    I. symbol for temporary and illusory
      happiness
    II. sign of the neighborhood's run-down
      condition
   III. source of background music
   A. I and III only   B. II and III only
   C. I, II, and III

9. Laura gives Jim the broken unicorn because   _____
   A. she doesn't want him to forget her

    B. she's grateful for his kindness
    C. she wants him to have a wedding gift

10. Tom refers to cities as "dead leaves" _____ because
    A. they have no meaning to him
    B. they have been destroyed by World War II
    C. Laura is not with him

11. Why is The Glass Menagerie an appropriate title for this play?

12. Does this play have a villain? Explain.

13. To what extent is Tom responsible for his "two-by-four situation"?

14. Laura recalls how self-conscious she felt in high school while "clumping up the aisle." How would you explain Jim's response that he "never even noticed"?

15. Which characters, if any, are better off at the end of the play than they were at the beginning?

ANSWERS

1. B	2. C	3. A	4. B	5. A	6. A
7. B	8. C	9. B	10. A		

11. Begin by assuming that the title *is* appropriate. The menagerie itself belongs to Laura and symbolizes her fragility. But since the collection gives the play its title, Laura's animals probably signify more. Think about the menagerie's other qualities. The animals are not real, for example; they are copies. One piece, the unicorn, doesn't even represent a real animal. Remember that the menagerie is not made of window glass. When you look through the little glass figures, everything appears distorted.

Additional qualities of the glass menagerie may occur to you: For instance, think of what glass does to light (makes rainbows), where the collection is located (on a shelf), and how it helps Laura escape from reality.

Can you describe Amanda and her family in similar terms? Are the Wingfields hardy, realistic people or are they apt to break easily? Do they view the world clearly and rationally? Do they lead "unreal" lives?

You might review the parts of this *Book Notes* which discuss character, setting and themes. In those sections you'll find more similarities between the glass menagerie and other aspects of the play. The more examples you cite, the more firmly you can assert that the title fits the play very snugly.

12. Not every work of literature has a villain, so start by defining the term. The definition will shape your answer.

The usual concept of a villain is someone (or something) whose deliberate actions bring harm to others. Most literary villains may have redeeming qualities, but readers ordinarily disapprove of villains. Using this definition, you may decide everyone in *The Glass Menagerie* has some villainous qualities. Tom, Laura, and Jim cause Amanda grief and worry. Amanda makes Tom suffer. Jim raises Laura's hopes and then dashes them. Tom selfishly abandons his family.

You might search beyond the characters to find your villain. Look to the circumstances of their lives. You could reasonably blame the social context for the plight of the Wingfields and Jim O'Connor. To support this position, read the numerous accounts of the time (the 1930's) and the place (St. Louis tenement) in the stage directions and in Tom's narration.

13. If you believe that Tom ought to bear responsibility for his own situation, try to show that he has deliberately chosen a dull, dead-end job. Also show that he purposely provokes Amanda and that he's too unimaginative and lazy to leave his rut. For example, you could argue that if Tom seriously aimed to be a poet, he should stay home and write rather than go to the movies every night.

Of course, Tom wouldn't be Tom if he did that, so you might conclude that Tom is partly a victim of circumstances. He thinks he can get himself out of his two-by-four situation, but he won't make the move—not until the end of the play. Family responsibility keeps him from breaking away. Also, his vision is limited. Another person might change his life without leaving home. But Tom thinks that the only way to change is by cutting his ties to Amanda and Laura.

A third choice—that Tom is trapped through no fault of his own—invites you to analyze Tom's personality and conditions of his family life. Tom has no choice about working. He's been stuck as the family breadwinner since his father left. During the Depression, people rarely quit jobs because new ones were hard to get. Also, Tom's conscience keeps him from walking out on his family. And regardless of his caged-in feeling, he loves Laura too much to leave her in the lurch.

14. This question calls for an exploration of Jim's past and present personality. How do you interpret Jim's response to Laura? Yes, Jim is polite. He takes pains to avoid wounding her. Further, his effort to boost her self-confidence will fail if he allows her to feel self-pity. So even if he had noticed her "clumping," is he likely to acknowledge it? Certainly he can be forgiven his little white lie.

Perhaps more to the point, though, is that he may be telling Laura the truth. Perhaps he *didn't* notice her clumping. Think of the sort of person Jim was in high school. He was blinded by his own glitter. Surrounded by admirers and absorbed by self-importance, would he have noticed Laura? Perhaps he is destined always to be saying, "I never even noticed."

Another interpretation: Laura's was a relatively mild defect and, like a roaring in one's ears, was really noticeable only to Laura. She made too much of it while others, even if they were aware of it at first, were ready to overlook it.

15. To some extent the four characters remain unchanged at the end of the play. Amanda continues to relive her youth, Laura still has no prospects for an independent future, Jim keeps pursuing elusive success, and Tom remains unfulfilled in his quest for adventure. In fact, you might argue that some characters are worse off. Laura, for one, after tasting a few moments of happiness may feel more hopeless than before.

On the other hand, if any character has realized something about life or about himself, that person has grown in some way. Consider Amanda. In the final scene she has "dignity and tragic beauty." You couldn't have described her that way at the start of the play. What has happened to her in the interim?

While Laura still has no suitor when the play ends, she has had a modest social triumph, however short-lived. Might the experience propel her out of her shell?

Tom could never be happy at home. Although he hasn't found the adventure he yearned for, is he better off for having tried?

Finally, Jim. There's little evidence to show that he was better off after his visit than before. However, his ego may have been boosted by Laura's admiration. Perhaps he has also become more sensitive to other people's feelings.

Term Paper Ideas and other Topics for Writing

Character Studies

1. What gives Tom the sense that he's in a "two-by-four" situation?

2. What are the apparent causes of Laura's removal from reality? What are the probable hidden causes?

3. If Tom were to write home after he leaves, what would he say to Amanda? To Laura?

4. If the play were in the memory of a character other than Tom, how would the play be different?

5. Who is the hero of the play? What evidence can you offer to support your opinion?

6. What are Amanda's strengths and failings as a mother?

Symbolism in the Play

1. Are the symbols for each character appropriate?

2. How do the play's symbols relate to its themes?

3. Compare and contrast symbolism in *The Glass Menagerie* with that in *A Streetcar Named Desire*.

The Play and its Meanings

1. How do the unconventional, anti-realistic production techniques contribute to the play's meanings?

2. In which ways does "memory" contribute to the mood of the play?

3. Is the ending of the play optimistic or pessimistic? Explain.

4. Discuss whether Tom's predicament is common or extraordinary.

5. What are the uses of illusion in everyday life? Do the play's characters use illusions in an unusual way?

6. To what degree is the play autobiographical?

A Streetcar Named Desire

THE PLAY

The Plot

Imagine a delicate white moth flitting about a heap of garbage in a cinder lot. That's approximately the feeling created by the sight of Blanche DuBois arriving in Elysian Fields to visit her sister Stella and brother-in-law Stanley Kowalski. Blanche not only looks out of place, she acts that way, too. Refinement and good breeding show in all she says and does, at least until her mask is stripped away bit by bit.

Blanche teaches high school English in Laurel, Mississippi. She needs a place to stay while recovering from a nervous breakdown. Stella agrees to accommodate Blanche, at least for a while, but she cautions Blanche that the apartment is tiny and that Stanley isn't the sort of man Blanche may be used to. He's rough and undignified. But Stella adores him despite his crude manner.

Soon after arriving, Blanche reveals that Belle Reve, the old family plantation in Laurel, has been lost to creditors. Blanche blames her sister for leaving home years ago while she was forced to stay on and watch all the residents of Belle Reve die off one by one.

The loss of Belle Reve troubles Stanley. He distrusts Blanche and accuses her of having sold the plantation to buy furs and jewels. When Blanche denies wrongdoing, Stanley ransacks her belongings looking for a bill of sale. He tears open a packet of letters and poems written by Blanche's husband, who committed suicide years ago. Stella tries unsuccessfully to protect her fragile sister from Stanley's fury.

That night Blanche and Stella go to the movies while Stanley and his friends play poker and drink. When they return, Blanche is introduced to Mitch, whose courteous manner sets him apart from Stanley's other friends. She charms Mitch easily and begins to flirt with him. Upset that the poker game has been interrupted, Stanley explodes in a drunken rage. He hurls a radio out the window and he strikes Stella. Spurred by Stanley's assault on his pregnant wife, his friends drag him into the shower. Meanwhile, Stella and Blanche escape upstairs to a friend's apartment.

Dripping wet, Stanley emerges into the street. Like an animal crying for his mate, he keeps calling Stella until she comes down and allows herself to be carried off to bed. Later Mitch returns and apologizes to Blanche for Stanley's coarse behavior.

Blanche is disgusted by Stanley's barbarity and would like to leave, but she has nowhere else to go. She invents a story about a rich friend named Shep Huntleigh who might give her refuge. She tries to persuade Stella to flee with her. However,

Stella rebuffs Blanche and pledges love for Stanley regardless of how brutally he treats her.

Mitch, a lonesome man in search of a wife, begins to date Blanche. But Stanley has acquired some information about her that would probably destroy the relationship. Stanley has learned that Blanche was an infamous whore back in Laurel. Blanche denies it, but soon after, when Blanche flirts with a newsboy, you realize that Stanley's assertion may be true.

Mitch talks of marriage. Blanche discloses the tragic story of her earlier marriage to Allan, who turned out to be a homosexual. When Blanche rejected him, Allan took his own life. Now Blanche can't erase from her mind the image of his bloody corpse or the sound of the fatal gunshot. Profoundly moved, Mitch embraces Blanche.

Stanley, meanwhile, has learned that Blanche hasn't taken a leave from her teaching job. Rather, she has been fired because she seduced one of her students. In addition, she was told to leave Laurel because night after night she entertained soldiers from a nearby army base.

Stanley tells Mitch about Blanche's past. As Stella prepares a birthday party for her sister, Stanley tells her, too. Shocked, Stella pleads with Stanley to be gentle with Blanche. But Stanley presents Blanche with a cruel birthday present—a one-way bus ticket back to Laurel. Stella rebukes Stanley for his heartlessness, but he reminds her that their marriage had liberated her from a life of phony gentility. Suddenly Stella feels labor pains and Stanley rushes her to the hospital.

That evening Mitch visits Blanche. He is highly

agitated and tells her what Stanley has said. She pleads for understanding by confessing that she had been intimate with men in order to fill her emptiness after Allan's suicide. Her tale arouses Mitch. He wants the sex that she's dispensed to others. He starts to assault her, but she repels him by shouting "Fire!" out the window.

Late that night Stanley returns to find Blanche dressed in fine traveling clothes. She informs Stanley that Shep Huntleigh has invited her on a cruise and that Mitch had apologized for not coming to her birthday party. Stanley bluntly calls her a liar. He wants to prove that he hasn't been fooled by her lies. He approaches her seductively. She tries to stop him with a bottle, but too weak to resist, she collapses at his feet. Stanley picks her up, then carries her off to be raped.

Weeks later Stella is packing Blanche's belongings. Blanche thinks that she's going to the country for a rest, but in truth, Blanche is being committed to a mental hospital. Stella doesn't know if she's doing the right thing. In order to preserve her marriage, however, Stella has decided to dismiss the story of the rape as just another of Blanche's fictions.

While dressing, Blanche talks of cruises and romantic adventures with Shep Huntleigh. Shortly, Stella leads Blanche out to meet the doctor and nurse from the hospital. Blanche balks at the sight of them. The nurse begins to overpower her with a straitjacket. But the doctor intervenes. He talks kindly to Blanche, as though he is the gentleman caller she's been expecting. Calmed by the doctor's gentleness, Blanche takes his arm and walks to the waiting ambulance.

The Characters

Blanche DuBois

Blanche is an English teacher, but she's one of a kind. You'd never forget her if you took her course. Shortly before the play begins, Blanche has lost her job. She wasn't fired for poor teaching skills, however. The superintendent's letter said Blanche was "morally unfit for her position." That's probably a fair evaluation of a teacher who seduced one of the seventeen-year-old boys in her class. Also, Blanche's sexual exploits so outraged the citizens of Laurel, Mississippi, that they practically threw her out of town.

You don't know all these facts about Blanche until late in the play. At first, she seems to be just a high-strung, but refined, woman who has come to New Orleans to pay her sister a visit. But as the play unfolds, you see Blanche's past revealed bit by bit. At the end she is undone, fit only for an asylum. Nevertheless, you never see her humbled by defeat. She maintains ladylike dignity even after being raped. Perhaps she's not as crazy as she appears. In fact, there might be places where she would not be regarded insane at all.

As an ambiguous character Blanche may arouse both compassion and disapproval simultaneously. She is often regarded as a symbol of a decaying way of life engaged in a losing struggle against modern commercialism. She came to Elysian Fields seeking love and help, but she found hostility and rejection. She has been scarred by her husband's suicide and by the loss of her ancestral home. She's reached a stage of life when she can no longer depend on her good looks to attract a man. Is it any wonder that she flirts and prefers dimly lit places?

To compensate for loneliness and despair, she creates illusions, much like Amanda Wingfield in *The Glass Menagerie*. Also like Amanda, Blanche clings to the manners and speech of dying Southern gentility. Pretending is important to her. It makes her feel special. She says that deception is half of a lady's charm. She calls it "magic." Unfortunately, though, she is caught in a situation with Stanley Kowalski, who not only abhors her superior airs, but seems bent on destroying her for them. Why Stanley finds Blanche such a threat is worth thinking about.

Some people consider Blanche not a tragic victim but an immoral woman who deserves what she gets. Blanche tells so many lies that she herself can't remember them all. Some lies may be harmless, but others are destructive. For example, Mitch is crushed by her untruthfulness.

Because of her past—town whore, liar, sexual deviate—you may agree with critics who say that Blanche is an object of derision—too degenerate to be taken seriously. On the other hand, her past behavior can be explained and maybe even defended. If you appreciate what has happened to her in life, you can understand why she acts the way she does.

In the end you may see Blanche as an advocate of civilized values. She alone speaks up for the nobility of humanity, for its achievements in the arts, for progress made by civilization. Are you struck by the irony of having uplifting words come from the mouth of an ex-prostitute? It is odd perhaps, but remember that Blanche often confuses truth and illusion. Perhaps Williams may be implying that society's most illustrious accomplishments are illusions, too, and that the brutish Stanley more accurately represents our true nature.

Stanley Kowalski

You always know where you stand with Stanley. He speaks plainly, he never hides his feelings, and he hates affectations of any kind. Yet in some respects he is a mystery. Why is he so intent on destroying Blanche? What makes him so aggressive? What was he like as a young man? How did he get to meet and court Stella? How does a man as animal-like as Stanley succeed as a traveling representative of his company? In short, is there more to Stanley than meets the eye?

You can only speculate. But sparse as the evidence is, you know he's a sturdy man of Polish descent, who likes to drink, play poker, and bowl. His greatest pleasure is sex. He also has a violent streak. He strikes Stella, hurls a radio out the window, throws dishes, shouts, and in uncontrollable fury, he rapes Blanche.

Yet, because of the actor Marlon Brando's original interpretation, Stanley is a brute with surprising appeal. Brando set the standard, making it difficult for later actors to reshape the role. Stanley can make you laugh at his earthy wit. His frankness is refreshing. There's no doubt about the power of his personality. He's always going to extremes, from his adoration of Stella to his self-centered pleasures.

Stanley's efforts to ruin Blanche reveal still other dimensions of his personality. Blanche not only interferes with his sex life, she attempts to lure Stella away from him. So his hatred of Blanche is quick and unrelenting. Perhaps you can respect Stanley for trying to defend his cave, but must he also destroy the intruder? Do you ravage a person merely for getting under your skin and cramping your style? Has Blanche really done anything to provoke Stanley's venom? Did she rob him of Belle Reve as he believes? Do Blanche's insults stir his hatred? What about Blanche's pretenses and perpetual lying?

Perhaps Stanley just can't tolerate the thought of being taken advantage of. If that's the case, he may mean no harm; he merely wants to protect his fragile ego and his way of life.

A further explanation of Stanley's malice toward Blanche may lie in the fact that they are a man and a woman. As a virile hunk of man Stanley is used to having his way with women. Blanche won't give him his way. But his discovery that she's been a whore is his ticket to tear away her pretenses, rape her, and bring her down to his level once and for all.

Stella Kowalski

If you didn't know that Blanche and Stella were sisters, could you guess that they were related? Both have a refinement that the other residents of Elysian Fields lack. They grew up together at Belle Reve. After the sisters reached adulthood Stella left for New Orleans, where she met and married Stanley.

What Stella might have become without Stanley is anybody's guess. She might have turned out like Blanche, trying futilely to maintain appearances and lying her way through life. Perhaps she would still be tied to the shabby gentility of the Old South because who but Stanley would have "pulled [her] down off them columns" on the plantation?

Stella is an unlikely mate for her brutal husband. She's a gentle woman of about twenty-five, level-headed and affectionate. Sex and bowling are the only interests she shares with him. When he plays poker, she goes to the movies. She accepts his tantrums, his abuses, and his coarse manners, perhaps the price she pays for having Stanley as a husband and a sex partner.

Stella seems to have the patience of a saint. When Blanche insults her, Stella often listens unperturbed, as though she is insensitive. But wouldn't you expect Stella to be hurt by Blanche's patronizing judgments? Why doesn't Stella fight back more often? Does she decline to defend herself because she has no ground for a defense, or could there be something else holding her back? Is Blanche's criticism too close to the painful truth? As Blanche berates her little sister, an unconscious hostility may be building inside Stella, something that may have begun years ago when the sisters were young. At the end of the play, when Stella commits Blanche to an asylum, you might regard Stella's action as her ultimate expression of antagonism toward her older sister.

Of course Stella may send Blanche away for her own good. She may prefer to believe that Blanche is insane rather than face the truth about Stanley. In effect, Stella chooses to sacrifice her sister rather than to destroy her marriage. Actually, it's uncertain whether Stella knows that Stanley raped Blanche. If she knows and closes her eyes to the fact, however, she is probably behaving true to form. Stella has learned a useful lesson from her older sister—how to deceive oneself to avoid coping with painful reality.

Harold Mitchell ("Mitch")

When Blanche meets Mitch, she is ready to turn her life around. Ordinarily, Blanche might have her eye out for a rich and courtly gentleman like the legendary Shep Huntleigh. Now she settles for Mitch, a good-hearted and honest fellow, but also a rather dull and self-conscious one.

Why is Blanche drawn to him? Obviously, it's not his awkward manner or stumbling speech that attracts her. Nor is it his short supply of intellect, money, wit, or looks. She is struck by his courtesy. He is the first person to treat her like a lady since her arrival in New Orleans. Second, he is an unmarried man. And his sense of propriety, in contrast to the other men in Stanley's poker-playing crowd of slobs, makes him stand out like a prince. He also happens to be lonely and is looking for someone to love.

Mitch is enthralled by Blanche the moment he sees her. She is clearly more refined, charming and intelligent than the women he's used to. He knows that his mother would approve. That's important to him. You rarely hear Mitch speak without mentioning his mother.

Blanche would be a good substitute for his mother. Blanche dominates Mitch, too, practically leading him around on a leash. He won't even kiss her without permission.

When you consider their personalities, what are the prospects for a successful match between Blanche and Mitch?

Stanley's revelations about Blanche's past put an end to the relationship. You don't see Mitch when he hears the truth about Blanche, but you can imagine his grief and shock.

Eunice Hubbell

The Hubbells own the building where the Kowalskis rent the first-floor apartment. Eunice and her husband live upstairs. Eunice pries into the daily lives of Stella and Stanley. You might call her nosy, or to be kind, neighborly. She probably deserves kindness because, like a big sister, she helps Stella in times of distress. For example, she gives refuge to Stella whenever Stanley goes on a rampage. The sounds that come from the Hubbells' apartment add to the jungle-like ambience of Elysian Fields and reveal that fighting and lovemaking are not restricted to the street floor of the building.

Eunice's comment to Stella about the rape of Blanche illustrates how Eunice, whose instincts are generally tender, has come to terms with the unspeakable vulgarity around her: "Don't ever believe it. Life has got to go on. No matter what happens, you've got to keep on going."

Steve Hubbell

Steve is one of Stanley's poker and drinking cronies. Like Stanley, he is crass and inelegant. He fights with his wife Eunice, throws dishes at her, and later, comes crawling back to her apologetically.

Pablo Gonzales

Pablo is the fourth member of Stanley's card-playing gang. Like the others, he is slovenly in mind and body.

A Young Collector

When he comes to collect for the newspaper he gets a kiss from Blanche instead of his fee. Blanche's encounter with the boy calls to mind two other boys in her experience: her young husband and the student in her English class whom she seduced.

Nurse and Doctor

They come to accompany Blanche to the asylum. The nurse, or matron, is just about to stuff Blanche into a straitjacket when the doctor, recognizing that a gentle hand is needed, steps in. Blanche rewards the doctor with thanks.

Other Elements

SETTING

Streetcar arrived on the stage in 1947. But don't assume that the story takes place in that year. Think of the story unfolding from May to September of any year you choose. It's true that Stanley and Mitch were army buddies in World War Two, but they could just as well be veterans of Vietnam or any other war.

The entire drama is played out on a single set. The street called Elysian Fields crosses the front of the stage. Through the transparent front wall of a shabby two-story structure, you see Stanley and Stella's flat, two rooms separated by a curtain. Beyond the apartment's rear wall, also transparent, you see the French Quarter of New Orleans.

Williams may have wanted you to feel that the drama enacted in the Kowalskis' flat was merely an extension of life in the city, and so he specified see-through walls in his stage directions. Outside you find railroad yards, a big water tank, empty lots and river docks—in short, nothing pretty or natural. In the characters you see another kind of ugliness: meanness, lying, hatred and more. Another possibility is that the transparent walls symbolize Williams' approach to the people in the play. It's not that you know them inside and out by the time the play ends, but that the characters' actions invite you to probe the inner workings of their hearts and minds.

Throughout the play you hear the sounds of the city. The tinny music of a "Blue Piano," suggesting sadness and lost love, recurs in several scenes. In addition, trains roar, radios blare, couples fight and make love. Windows and doors are kept open all summer, blurring the distinction between inside and outside. Stanley and his friends seem to have erased that distinction from their lives, too. Like animals in heat, they lack inhibition. Stanley especially lets it all hang out. He says whatever he thinks, regardless of the consequences.

If you know New Orleans you know the French Quarter. It's an historic section of the city, a hive of narrow streets, alleyways, markets, coffeehouses, honky-tonks and shops of all kinds. It's known for its quaint charm. Elaborate wrought-iron balconies laced with flowers extend from the facades of numerous buildings. Some of the residents may live in squalor, but they put up a pretty front. In a sense, they may remind you of Blanche DuBois.

THEMES

The following are themes of *A Streetcar Named Desire.*

1. THE VICTORY OF THE APES

One of Blanche's impassioned speeches to Stella depicts Stanley as an ape. It's true, there is something apelike about him. You see his primitive qualities from the first moment of the play, when he comes home lugging a package of bloody meat.

Stay alert throughout the play for many allusions to the subhuman quality of life in Elysian Fields. Sometimes the place is described as a jungle. Shrieks and groans pierce the hot, humid air. Mitch is described as a bear, the women are called "hens." Stanley and Stella emit *"low, animal moans."*

Blanche is the only champion for civilization in the play. "Don't hang back with the brutes!" she tells Stella. What conclusion can be drawn from the fact that the brutes ultimately destroy her? Are Blanche's values useless in a savage world?

2. LONELINESS

Loneliness is a fearful plague. Look at what it's done to Blanche. Bereft after her husband's suicide, she became a prostitute to fill her emptiness. She molests young boys and has constructed a web of pretense to delude herself and others that she is charming and sociable. She invents tales about her gentleman friend Shep Huntleigh. Whether he's a real or an imaginary person isn't important. He is real enough to comfort Blanche and to keep hope alive that someday she'll be rescued from loneliness.

The pain of loneliness brings Blanche and Mitch together. No doubt Blanche prefers men of another stripe, but rather than remain a lonely spinster for the rest of her life, she's willing to put up with him. Mitch, too, hopes to find a woman to replace his mother, who will soon die.

3. INVENTING A BEAUTIFUL PAST

When most of us glance back to the past, we wear rose-colored glasses, and if the present is bleak, the past appears still rosier. In *Streetcar*, hardly a character is immune from visions of a beautiful past.

Blanche's manner and way of speaking suggest the sort of past she has lodged in her memory. You'd think she grew up in grandeur and gentility of the Old South, at least until you hear her tell Stella the history of Belle Reve's decline. Why does Stella recall the white-columned plantation with fondness? Would she have left the place at an early age if life there had been so attractive? The name *Belle Reve* (beautiful dream) indicates, perhaps, that both Blanche and Stella believe in an illusion.

4. REALITY VS ILLUSION

In symbolic terms, the conflict between Stanley and Blanche pits reality against illusion. What is reality? To Stanley reality is what you can touch and see. Stanley feels right at home in reality—that is, among *real* people, the kind who act natural and who say what they think and feel. Since a human is an animal, according to Stanley he ought to act like one. To put on airs, to deny one's instincts, to hide one's feelings—those are dishonest acts.

No wonder Blanche rejects reality in favor of illusion. Reality has treated her unkindly. Too much truthfulness destroyed her marriage. Taking refuge in dreams and illusions, therefore, she plays a perpetual game of let's pretend. She says what *ought* to be true, not what *is* true.

Stanley can't tolerate idealists like Blanche. What

she calls "magic" Stanley calls "lies." Losing her way altogether at the end of the play, Blanche can no longer distinguish illusion from reality. So she goes to an asylum, the only place where that distinction doesn't make any difference.

5. SEXUAL VIOLENCE

The proverbial conflict between males and females has often been termed the "battle of the sexes." Sexual hostilities rage throughout the play. On one side you have Blanche, who is a veteran of considerable sexual give and take. She lures the newspaper boy into her arms, but thinks the better of it, and frees him after only one kiss. She wins Mitch's affection but claims "high ideals" to keep him at a distance. When Mitch discovers that he's been hoodwinked, he attempts to rape her. Blanche wards off the attack like a seasoned warrior.

Only Stanley is unconquerable. He sees right through Blanche's sexual pretenses. At the end of his war with Blanche, he rapes her, proving that in sexual combat, he is the winner and still champion.

STYLE

This play about people trapped in frightful conditions brims with poetry. A poem doesn't always need elegant words. In fact, the inelegant residents of Elysian Fields speak in the blunt, straightforward idiom of common people. Only Blanche's manner of speaking soars above the ordinary. Figurative language gushes naturally from her lips. For example, she tells Mitch how life's joys have been extinguished: "And then the searchlight which had been turned on the world was turned off again and never for one moment since has there been any light that's stronger than this—kitchen—candle. . . ." Why did Williams give Blanche the gift of poetic speech? Yes, she's an English teacher, but perhaps he had other purposes. How does her eloquence affect her relationship with Stanley, for instance?

You also find poetic language, rich with imagery, in Williams' stage directions: *"The houses [of New Orleans] are mostly white frame, weathered grey, with rickety outside stairs and galleries and quaintly ornamented gables."* To help create the mood of the play, Williams prescribes the sound of a *"tinny piano being played with the infatuated fluency of brown fingers."* To give you a sense of the character, he calls Stanley a *"gaudy seed bearer"* and a *"richly feathered male bird among hens."* Blanche's uncertain manner, as well as her white clothes, suggest *"a moth."*

Apes, hens, a moth—Williams' images make up a menagerie. Why does the playwright repeatedly compare his characters to animals? Does Williams keep you mindful of the constant tension between man's civilized impulses and his beast-like instincts?

The playwright may also be highlighting the symbolic clash between Stanley and Blanche. To be sure, Stanley stands for primitivism. Blanche speaks up for civilization. May she also represent the romantic traditions of the past? Don't be satisfied with only those interpretations of Stanley and Blanche. Try to extract additional symbolic meanings in the conflict between the play's antagonists. For example, what can you make of the fact that one is a dreamer and pretender, the other a realist?

You're always sure to find carefully-chosen symbols in a Williams play. Even the names of people and places carry symbolic weight. The streetcars, "Desire" and "Cemetery," evoke among other things, Blanche's need for love and her fear of death. Other names reveal Williams' irony and humor: he assigns the name "Elysian Fields," a paradise in ancient mythology, to a cheerless street in modern New Orleans. "Blanche" means white, the color signifying purity. "Stella," the earthy sister, means star. And "Belle Reve," of course, means "beautiful dream."

POINT OF VIEW

Unlike *The Glass Menagerie*, *A Streetcar Named Desire* has no narrator to tell you the story. No one comes between you and the characters on the stage. The story is presented as it is in most plays—by characters simply playing their parts. What the characters represent, how they interact, how they resolve conflicts all help to establish the playwright's point of view.

In the script of the play Williams includes plenty of material that describes the set, the appearance of the characters, the sound and light needed to create moods and so forth. But he doesn't tell you how to view the characters: Is Blanche sane or insane? Does Stanley have redeeming qualities? Is it right for Stella to commit Blanche to an asylum? Although these are questions that Williams probably wants you to answer for yourself, he gives you his own bias by focusing the play on Blanche.

Blanche stands apart as the central figure. *Streetcar* is her story, and you have a ringside seat to her private agony and disintegration. You never see anyone except Blanche on stage alone. Minor characters like the newsboy and the flower peddler are interesting only insofar as they touch Blanche. By the time the play ends you know Blanche better than any other character. You probably understand why she acts as she does and appreciate what has happened to her. That doesn't mean you cherish her. But you might feel compassion for her, as you might for anyone who has lost her way.

How you feel about Blanche and how you interpret her actions will ultimately determine your views not only about the other characters, but about the themes and ideas conveyed by the play as a whole.

FORM AND STRUCTURE

Most plays have acts. *Streetcar* doesn't. Rather it is divided into eleven scenes occurring in chronological order and taking place between May and September.

In most productions of a play, you'll find intermissions at natural breaks in the action. In many productions of *Streetcar*, intermissions come after Stanley has won his first major victory over Blanche, at the end of Scene Four. A second break sometimes occurs when Scene Six concludes, after Blanche has won Mitch's love. Thus, the first third of the play ends with a defeat for Blanche, the second with a triumph.

The last scenes follow Blanche's decline into permanent defeat—her insanity. You might observe a kind of rhythm in the action of the play, a pulsing series of episodes, which may explain why Williams chose to build the play using several short scenes instead of a few longer acts. There's a rhythm of conflict and reconciliation: Stanley and Stella have a row, then make up. Eunice and Steve fight, then make up. Blanche, as usual, is out of step with the others. She establishes a liaison with Mitch, which then breaks up. Perhaps the regularity of the pattern is meant to suggest vaguely the rhythm of passion, which reaches a climax in the rape scene. The suggestion becomes more plausible if you think of the play as a sexual battle between Stanley and Blanche.

A Streetcar Named Desire is episodic. A drawing of the play's structure traces the conflict between Blanche and Stanley and also parallels the state of Blanche's emotional and mental health.

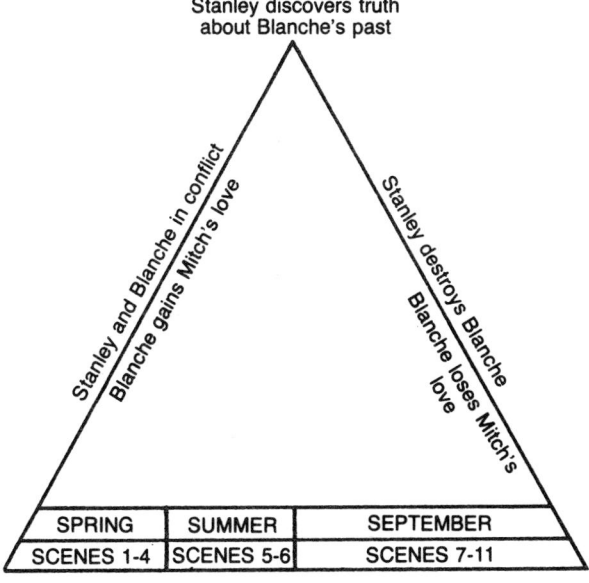

SPRING	SUMMER	SEPTEMBER
SCENES 1-4	SCENES 5-6	SCENES 7-11

Scene 1: Blanche arrives in New Orleans, meets

Stanley; each takes the other's measure. Blanche generally optimistic.

Scene 2: Conflict over loss of Belle Reve. Blanche submits papers to Stanley.

Scene 3: Poker night. Blanche meets Mitch. Blanche hopeful about the future.

Scene 4: Blanche berates Stella. Stanley defeats Blanche in competition for Stella's allegiance.

Scene 5: Blanche plans for future; she kisses newsboy. Blanche hopes that Mitch will provide love.

Scene 6: Date with Mitch. Blanche wins Mitch's love.

Scene 7: Preparation for party. Blanche in high spirits.

Scene 8: Stanley gives Blanche bus ticket; Blanche horrified.

Scene 9: Mitch visits Blanche, attempts rape. Blanche distraught.

Scene 10: Stanley returns; rapes Blanche. Blanche destroyed.

Scene 11: Blanche sent to insane asylum.

The Play

SCENE ONE

At the start of *A Streetcar Named Desire*, Tennessee Williams paints a loving portrait of New Orleans.

NOTE: Williams spent several months in the city before writing the play. He lived in a flat overlooking the streetcar tracks where one car named *Desire* and another called *Cemetery* ran back and forth every day. Somehow the names of the streetcars and their ceaseless comings and goings struck his poetic mind with "having some symbolic bearing of a broad nature on the life in the [French Quarter]—and everywhere else, for that matter. . . ."

Like April in Paris, May in New Orleans is one of those legendary times of year. The air is warm but not yet thick with summer heat. Brilliant flowers sprout on sills and terraces. Open doors and windows blur the distinctions between sidewalk and living room. You walk down the street in the French Quarter and hear the sounds of a jazz piano and the voices of the people. The smells are sweet from cargoes of coffee and bananas in freighters along the river.

Williams' affection for the place extends even to the run-down section of town between the railroad tracks and the waterfront. There, you find a street named Elysian Fields.

NOTE: The name comes from Greek myth. Elysium was a happy land, a paradise free from rain, snow, cold or misfortune of any kind. When you get further into the play you'll doubtlessly recognize the irony in Williams' choices of names.

Stanley Kowalski comes on stage first, walking with his friend Mitch. He is a hulk of a man carrying a package of bloody meat, which he heaves to his wife Stella, standing on the first floor landing. Williams probably wants you to imagine Stanley as a modern caveman, returning to his mate with the kill for the day. Instead of wearing a leopard skin, however, he's carrying a bowling jacket. Stanley tells Stella that he's on his way to bowl and she, his faithful mate, follows him to the alley.

Shortly after Stella leaves, Blanche DuBois, carrying a suitcase, hesitantly walks down Elysian Fields. From her gestures and her clothing you can tell instantly that she is a stranger. She looks as though she ought to be headed for a summer tea party in the garden district instead of searching for the rickety, two-story building occupied by the Kowalskis.

As soon as she speaks—to ask directions from Eunice Hubbell, the Kowalskis' upstairs neighbor—you can be sure that Blanche is used to more refined surroundings. Despite Blanche's doubts that Stella really lives in such a place, Eunice assures her that she's found the right address. When Blanche discloses she is Stella's sister, Eunice escorts Blanche into the apartment. Eunice wants to chat, but Blanche asks to be left alone, claiming to be tired from her trip. As she leaves, Eunice offers to tell Stella of Blanche's arrival.

Until now you have no reason to doubt that Blanche is anything other than what you've observed and heard: a worn-out traveler from Mississippi where she teaches school and owns her family's ancestral home, Belle Reve, a large plantation with a white-columned mansion.

As soon as Eunice goes out, however, you watch Blanche, apparently upset and nervous about something, find whiskey in a closet and quickly swallow half a glassful. Then she mutters to herself, "I've got to keep hold of myself!"

Whatever has caused Blanche's agitation begins to unfold soon after Stella returns. Blanche chatters at a feverish pace. As she speaks, she reveals her unsettled emotional state. In just a brief dialogue with her sister, Blanche expresses affection, shock, modesty, concern for Stella, vanity, resentment, and uncertainty about herself. While almost every sentence reveals another dimension of Blanche's inner turbulence, the dialogue also illustrates the relationship between the sisters.

Blanche explains that she has suffered a nervous breakdown and has therefore taken a leave from her teaching job in the middle of the term. Blanche then disparages Stella's messy apartment and reproaches Stella for gaining so much weight. (Blanche does not know that Stella is pregnant.)

Stella almost apologizes for the size of her apartment. She also starts to prepare Blanche for meeting Stanley and his friends. They're not exactly the type of men Blanche is accustomed to. Perhaps Stella already realizes that Stanley and Blanche are not going to get along. They come from two different worlds. Since Stella came originally from the same landed gentry as Blanche, she somehow must have leapt across a social chasm, for now Stella worships Stanley despite his rough cut. She admits that much of his appeal is sexual.

Blanche finally turns the conversation to news of home. She fears telling it, just as anyone might shrink, say, from bearing the grievous news of a loved one's death. Blanche announces that Belle Reve has been lost. Before Stella can ask why, Blanche launches into a passionate and morbid apology which assigns blame for the loss on a parade of sickness and death that marched through the family. Every death had to be paid for with a little piece of Belle Reve, and gradually the place just slipped away through Blanche's fingers.

More shocked than angry, Stella says nothing. Blanche thinks that Stella doubts the story and cruelly lashes out at her sister: "Yes, accuse me! Sit there and stare at me, thinking I let the place go! *I* let the place go? Where were *you!* In bed with your—Polack!"

Blanche's attack on Stella suggests the intensity of her feelings about the loss. On the other hand, she could be covering up the facts, possibly to protect herself, possibly because she can't face the truth. Unable to accept responsibility, she may be casting blame on the dead people in her family and ultimately on her little sister, all characters, take note, without the capacity to defend themselves.

NOTE: It takes a particularly skillful actress to play Blanche. She possesses many villainous qualities. In this scene you have observed her being cruel, bossy, hypocritical and dishonest. Yet, the actress who portrays her must preserve the goodwill of the audience. If you didn't like Blanche at least a little, her struggle with Stanley, which is about to begin, would be far less compelling than it is.

When Stella runs to the bathroom in tears, Stanley and friends, Steve and Mitch, return from bowling and plan a poker game for the following evening. You see that Stanley easily lives up to Stella's description. He is crude and animal like, but he knows his sexual attractiveness and uses it unsparingly.

Notice how Stanley treats Blanche during their first encounter. Is there any apparent reason for him to be nasty to her? Does he simply lack grace? Or has he just taken an instant dislike to Blanche? Perhaps her airs annoy him. Perhaps he can't tolerate Blanche's prattling about looking fresh and powdering her face. Because Stella has told him about her sister, Stanley may long ago have made up his mind to dislike her. It's also possible that Stanley, like an animal smelling danger, senses that Blanche may come between him and his mate in their small living quarters.

Finally, when Stanley asks about her marriage, Blanche cannot talk about it with him. Is the subject too painful? Or does she have something to hide? You'll find out later, but for the moment, she feels too sick to continue.

SCENE TWO

It's poker night at the Kowalskis. Stella plans to take Blanche on the town to get her out of the house while Stanley and his cronies drink beer and play for modest stakes.

While Blanche soaks in the tub Stella urges Stanley to be kind to Blanche. Stanley ignores Stella's pleas. He wants to know more about the loss of Belle Reve. He can't understand that the place is just—gone! He wants to see a bill of sale or papers of some kind to confirm Blanche's story. He cites the Napoleonic Code that says what belongs to the wife also belongs to the husband and vice versa. If Belle Reve is gone, it's his loss as well as Stella's.

NOTE: Stanley is right. Because the Louisiana Territory was owned by France before President Thomas Jefferson bought it for the United States, French civil law, the so-called *Code Napoléon,* was used for a long time to govern Louisiana's civil affairs. In the Code you find rules about inheritance and property. In recent years, however, the Code has gradually been superseded by new laws and court decisions.

Stanley suspects that Blanche used the money from Belle Reve to deck herself in furs and jewels and costly dresses. In defense of Blanche, Stella tells him that the furs are cheap and the jewelry is fake, but Stanley refuses to let the matter rest.

Taking Blanche's side could not be easy for Stella, yet she stands up for her sister. She may believe Blanche's story. Or perhaps Blanche's nervous condition has aroused Stella's sympathy. In either case, Stella is caught in the middle. Before Blanche emerges from the bathroom, Stella escapes to the porch, leaving Stanley to face Blanche alone.

Not suspecting what is in store, Blanche comes out of the bathroom and banters cheerfully with Stanley. She plays the role of coquette, flaunting her helplessness and fishing for compliments. But he is wise to her flirtatious antics, and she is not impressed with his brutishness. Considering his sexual power, he may also be testing the water. Does she have the strength to resist him? He probably would like to find out.

Blanche could probably go on all day, but Stanley grows impatient with the chatter. Suddenly he booms out "Now let's cut the re-bop!" He **wants** to know the truth about Belle Reve. When **he** cites the Napoleonic Code to Blanche, she taunts **him,** "My, but you have an impressive judicial **air!**" She sprays him with perfume, teasing him **some more.** Her seductive manner drives him to say **that** he'd get the wrong ideas about her if she wasn't Stella's sister. The remark sobers her a little. **She** grants that while she may fib a little, she **wouldn't** lie about something as important as Belle **Reve.** She'll show the papers to Stanley if he wants **to see** them.

Impatient for the papers, Stanley **grabs** for them inside Blanche's trunk. What he **finds** is a packet of love letters and poems written **by** Blanche's **late** husband, Allan. Blanche refers to her husband **as** a "boy." It's a curious usage. Blanche and he **were** married when both were very young. Allan **died** before he reached manhood. In another sense, Allan lacked the qualities to be considered a man in the fullest sense of the term. You'll find out why further in the play. In any event, Blanche treasures his letters and vows to burn them now that Stanley's hands have touched them.

Finally, she hands Stanley a towering pack of legal papers that span the history of Belle Reve. This time, Blanche attributes the loss of the plantation not to the numerous deaths that occurred there, but to the "epic fornications" of generations of DuBois men. Stanley is befuddled by the mass of papers. Perhaps Blanche was telling the truth after all. He explains his interest in Stella's welfare, especially now that she's going to have a baby.

The news of Stella's baby stirs Blanche. She rushes out to find Stella and to tell her that she and Stanley have settled their differences. Blanche brags that she conquered Stanley with wit and a bit of flirting. But you'll notice that her triumph over Stanley is mostly wishful thinking. If he were to retell what happened during this scene, the story would probably be a lot different.

NOTE: You might think of *A Streetcar Named Desire* as a modern equivalent of a classic tragedy, in which you follow the suffering and gradual defeat of a person who probably doesn't deserve it. As the hero fights to survive he cannot keep from sinking further into hopelessness and despair. It seems as though his fate has been predetermined. As you continue the play, try to discern other similarities between Blanche and a typical tragic hero.

SCENE THREE

The poker game is still underway when Blanche and Stella return from their night out. Stanley, on a losing streak, lashes out at Mitch for wanting to go home. He also snaps at Blanche, whacks Stella on the thigh, and orders the two women to leave the men to their game.

Alone with Stella in the other room, Blanche observes that Mitch had seemed noticeably more courteous and sensitive than the other men. When Blanche and Stella laugh aloud, Stanley shouts, "You hens cut out that conversation in there." But Stella protests. In her house she'll do as she pleases.

Does it seem as though a row is about to begin? When Blanche turns on the radio, Stanley demands that it be turned off. When she refuses, he does it himself. The poker players, like nervous animals before a storm, become restless with Stanley's antics. When Mitch drops out of the game, Blanche seizes the chance to talk with him. Observe Blanche in conversation with Mitch. She's a study in deception. She knows just how to charm him. She talks of the beauty of sick people. (Stella has told her that Mitch is devoted to his sick mother.) She playfully slurs some words, pretending to be slightly drunk. She tells him that Stella is her older sister (a lie), and that Stella's need for help has brought her to town (another lie).

Blanche asks Mitch to cover a naked light bulb with a colored paper lantern, bought earlier that evening. Mitch obliges, unaware of Blanche's intention to hide her real age and, when you consider her other deceptions, perhaps a lot more than that. At any rate, Blanche's wiles work on Mitch. He is won over instantly, hypnotized by her charm.

Blanche clicks on the radio. You hear a beautiful waltz. Caught up in the music, Blanche dances gracefully. Mitch imitates her awkwardly, like a dancing bear.

NOTE: The waltz, *Wien, Wien, nur du allein,* is a sentimental expression of love for old-time Vienna, the city of dreams. The song conjures up images of elegance and splendor that contrast with the run-down apartment of the Kowalskis. Ironically, at the time *A Streetcar Named Desire* was written the beauty of Vienna existed only as a memory. The city lay in ruins from heavy bombing during the war. Watch for other discrepancies between reality and illusion in the play.

Stanley, in a rage, stalks into the room, grabs

the radio and throws it out the window. Then he charges Stella and strikes her. Before he can land another blow, the other men rush forward and pin his arms behind him. He suddenly becomes limp, as though exhausted by his tantrum. To sober him up, his friends drag him to the shower.

Meanwhile, Blanche, distraught and frightened, has organized a hasty escape upstairs to Eunice's with Stella in tow.

Soon Stanley emerges dripping. Somehow his meanness has vanished. Now he's like a vulnerable little boy almost in tears, crying for his baby, his Stella. Half dressed, he stumbles outside to the front pavement and howls again and again, "Stella! Stella!" Eunice warns him to leave her alone, but after a time Stella comes out the door and slips down the stairs to Stanley. The two embrace. Stanley then lifts her and carries her into the dark flat.

Does it surprise you to see Stella return to Stanley so soon after he abused her? Obviously, she loves him desperately. Perhaps she is aroused by Stanley's bestiality.

NOTE: Williams learned a good deal about uninhibited sexuality from the writings of the English novelist D. H. Lawrence (1885–1930). An artist-rebel, Lawrence scorned conventional sexual behavior. Williams, himself a sexual nonconformist, admired both Lawrence and his work. One of Williams' plays, *I Rise in Flame, Cried the Phoenix*, is based on the last days of Lawrence's life.

Blanche seems shaken by Stanley's outburst.

Mitch returns and tries to comfort her. Together, they smoke a cigarette. Apparently still dazed and confused by what she had witnessed, Blanche thanks Mitch for his kindness.

SCENE FOUR

The next morning Stella, tired but evidently content after a night of love, lies peacefully in bed. Blanche expresses dismay over last night's brawl, but Stella objects. It's scarcely worth speaking of. Anyway, all is forgiven because Stanley felt ashamed afterwards.

Stella admits to her sister that Stanley's brutish manner appeals to her. In fact, it's rather thrilling. Stella recounts the excitement of her wedding night when Stanley charged around the apartment breaking lightbulbs with the heel of her shoe. How might Blanche have reacted in a like situation?

You've already seen Blanche treating Stella tactlessly. But now she becomes downright cruel. Stanley is a madman, she says, and if Stella had any sense, she'd leave him immediately.

To understand Stella, you might ask why she chooses to stay with her ill-tempered husband. Is she a model of broad-mindedness? Or is she a weakling? Or has she become a fatalist, that is, someone who just accepts her lot in life? As you'll see later, Stella's personality and values will help to seal Blanche's fate.

Blanche urges Stella to come away with her. She proposes opening a shop of some kind with money provided by Shep Huntleigh, a rich acquaintance. Although Shep may be only a figment of her imagination, Blanche starts to write him a telegram:

"Sister and I in desperate situation. . . ." In truth, of course, the despair is all Blanche's.

For Stella most of life's anxieties and troubles are made trivial by what she calls the "things that happen between a man and a woman in the dark." Stella calls it love, but Blanche terms it "brutal desire" and begins to address Stella on the subject of Stanley's bestiality. Blanche, as though a spokesman for civilization, talks of man's noble accomplishments in art and poetry. All that, she says, has passed Stanley by. Blanche ends with a passionate plea: *"Don't—don't hang back with the brutes!"*

NOTE: Blanche's speech illustrates one of the play's major conflicts, a symbolic clash between civilization and barbarism. By the end of the scene, you'll be able to chalk up a victory for one of them.

After Blanche finishes, Stanley reveals that he'd overheard the whole conversation. Stella's moment of decision has come. Will she be swayed by Blanche's eloquence? Stanley's grin of triumph, flashed at Blanche over Stella's shoulder, suggests that it was really no contest.

SCENE FIVE

To keep her hope alive, or at least to keep up the pretense of hope, Blanche composes a letter to Shep Huntleigh, informing him that she intends to make room in her crowded social life to visit him in Dallas.

NOTE: Regardless of whether Shep is imaginary or real, to Blanche he represents a chance to be rescued from her plight. He's a savior, a symbol of a vanishing breed—the gallant, romantic, and wealthy Southern gentleman. More than likely, such a man is Blanche's mirage. Earlier you heard her rage against the real Southern gentlemen she knew.

While Blanche reads a piece of the letter to Stella, you hear angry shouts and curses from upstairs. Steve and Eunice are embroiled in one of their periodic arguments. Later they make up and, like Stella and Stanley after the poker game, clasp each other fiercely. Have you noticed the characters' fluctuating emotions? Rapidly, their joy may turn to anger or anger to joy. They hit emotional peaks and valleys in swift succession. Could these fluctuations signify the characters' instability? Or do they suggest, as some critics have noted, the rhythms of sexual passion?

Some time after, Stanley startles Blanche by mentioning a certain man named Shaw from Laurel. Shaw claims to have met a woman named Blanche at Laurel's Hotel Flamingo, a seedy place frequented by the town's lowlife. Stanley stops short of calling Blanche a whore, but he strongly implies that Blanche is something other than an English teacher. Blanche denies it, of course, but nervousness gives her away.

While Blanche might like Stella as a confidante, someone to whom she can unburden herself, it's not a role Stella savors. However, Blanche asks Stella for advice about Mitch, soon to arrive for another evening out. Like a young girl just starting to date, Blanche asks how freely she can grant sexual favors and still retain her beau's respect. For a teenager the question is a puzzlement. For a grown woman, whose career includes a spell as town whore, the problem is both comic and tragic, but important nevertheless.

NOTE: The further you explore the play, the more psychological turns and byways you'll discover. By now the play has turned almost into a psychological drama, recalling works by Chekhov, the Russian playwright, who let characters unveil their mental processes without help from a narrator or from the remarks of other characters. You understand the inner being of characters almost solely from the words they say. In his later years Tennessee Williams often acknowledged Chekhov's influence on his work.

Soon after Stella and Stanley leave for the evening, a boy of about high school age comes to collect for the newspaper. Blanche makes advances. She flirts with him, and finally, to the boy's astonishment, plants a kiss on his mouth. Afterwards she mutters, "It would be nice to keep you, but I've got to be good—and keep my hands off children." Blanche says the words as though she's recalling her past, suggesting perhaps that she's had encounters with children before.

Why does she kiss the young man? Is she a sexual deviant? Does the encounter make her feel young? Is she testing her seductive powers? Later, after you learn more about Blanche's past, you might develop additional theories. Similarly, you might ponder the boy's response. Was he stunned with surprise? Did he submit out of courtesy?

Blanche's brush with the boy has buoyed her morale. Moments later, Mitch arrives bearing a bouquet of roses. Coquettishly she presses the flowers to her lips and calls Mitch her "Rosenkavalier."

NOTE: The central moment in the Richard Strauss opera *Der Rosenkavalier* is the presentation of a silver rose to a beautiful young woman. The allusion certainly goes way over Mitch's head, but he catches the spirit of Blanche's words and smiles appreciatively.

SCENE SIX

It's two a.m., and Blanche and Mitch are returning from an evening out. The streets are empty. Even the streetcars have stopped. However, Blanche asks Mitch whether "Desire" is still running. She's teasing him, inquiring about the state of his desire—presumably for her. You may understand Blanche's subtle joke, but Mitch doesn't.

NOTE: "Desire" carried Blanche to Elysian Fields. The other streetcar was "Cemetery." Such names may allude remotely to the excessive desire and string of deaths that led to the loss of Belle Reve. In another sense, Blanche *desires* to find beauty in life. If she loses the desire, she might as well be dead. By the end of the play, other explanations may become apparent.

Blanche and Mitch sit on the steps outside the building. Would he be a suitable mate for Blanche? Probably not, but Blanche can't be particular at this point in life. Mitch is a man, and that's what she wants. Now you see Blanche deftly baiting a trap. Mitch is easy prey for her. But she has to make him believe that he's caught her, not vice versa.

Blanche seems to enjoy toying with Mitch. At one point overconfidence almost gives her away. She laughs cynically at Mitch's sincerely meant, but prosaic, declaration, "I have never known anyone like you."

Inside the apartment, Blanche lights a candle instead of turning on the light. Whimsically, she suggests they pretend to be Parisian artists. In French, Blanche says, "I am the Lady of the Camellias, and you are Armand."

NOTE: Blanche, speaking in French, surely knows that Mitch has no idea what she's talking about. The Lady of the Camellias is a courtesan in a 19th-Century novel by Alexandre Dumas fils. Her lover Armand reforms her, but before long she dies of consumption. Giuseppe Verdi's famous opera *La Traviata* is based on the story.

Also in French, Blanche asks, "Will you sleep with me tonight?" Poor Mitch! He doesn't understand that Blanche is making a fool of him. But is she being unkind to him? Or is she just having a bit of innocent fun?

Blanche feigns interest as he describes gym workouts and the firmness of his stomach muscles. Mocking him, Blanche says that his body-weight is "awe-inspiring." You might feel sorry for Mitch. After all, he's not at fault for being something of a buffoon. Although he's a grown man, he's still under his mother's wing. When Mitch reveals that his mother asked to know Blanche's age, you can be sure that marriage is on his mind.

Before she accepts a proposal, Blanche needs to be sure that Mitch knows nothing about Shaw and about her soiled reputation. If Stanley were to tell him . . . well, you can see why she ominously calls Stanley her "executioner."

Possibly to win Mitch's sympathy, Blanche relates the story of her marriage. It's a tragic tale of love, homosexuality, and violence. It's hard not to feel moved by it. All of a sudden you understand Blanche far better than before. She's tortured by guilt about her husband's death.

The story brings Mitch close to tears. Realizing that Blanche is as lonely as he, Mitch takes her in his arms and kisses her. Blanche sobs in relief. She's worked hard to land Mitch, and in triumph, declares "Sometimes—there's God—so quickly!"

SCENE SEVEN

After four months Blanche and Stanley are still at odds. Is there any doubt which of them will win in the end?

Stella is setting up for Blanche's birthday celebration when Stanley comes home elated. "I've got th' dope on your big sister, Stella," he says. A supply man who's been driving through Laurel for years has told him the X-rated story of Blanche DuBois. Her daintiness and squeamish ways are nothing but a big act.

Stella refuses to believe the outrageous story, but Stanley insists that Blanche had been told to leave town for being a hotel whore and for seducing one of the seventeen-year-old boys in her class.

As Stanley tells the story, Blanche soaks in the tub and cheerfully sings "Paper Moon," a pop tune about a world that's "as phony as it can be."

NOTE: The stage directions often prescribe playing background music that relates to the action. In Scene Six, as Blanche recalled her husband's suicide, you heard "The Varsouviana" a polka that was played at the Moon Lake Casino on the night Allan shot himself. You'll soon hear it again.

Stella urges Stanley to be kind to Blanche, who needs understanding because of her tragic marriage. But Stanley won't relent. Moreover, he's already informed Mitch about Blanche's sordid past. Stanley claims that he felt obliged to warn Mitch that Blanche is a fraud, but you might suspect other reasons for his action.

Blanche's marriage to Mitch is now out of the question. To compound the injury, Stanley has bought Blanche a bus ticket back to Laurel. What's to become of Blanche, Stella wonders. Stanley's answer shows how little he cares.

Emerging from the bathroom, Blanche reads distress on Stella's face, but Stella won't disclose the reason. That task belongs to Stanley.

SCENE EIGHT

Naturally, Mitch doesn't show up for the birthday dinner. Blanche tries vainly to keep up her spirits and tells a joke. Stella laughs weakly, but Stanley remains stone faced. As he reaches across the table for another chop, Stella calls him a "pig." She orders him to wash his greasy face and fingers and to help her clear the table.

Stanley throws his plate and cup on the floor. "That's how I'll clear the table!" he bellows.

NOTE: Audiences watching *Streetcar* often laugh at Stanley's table-clearing technique. While Stanley's action contains humor, it also has its frightening aspect. When he allows himself to be dominated by violence, he has the potential to do unspeakable damage.

Stanley berates Stella. Since Blanche arrived, he's been a second-class member of his own household. As you watch Stanley reclaim his position as "king" of the roost, he reveals that he's embittered by the wedge that Blanche has placed between him and Stella. Perhaps you can sympathize with him on that score.

After Stanley stalks out, Blanche tries to phone Mitch to find out why he stood her up. Meanwhile, Stella goes to Stanley on the porch and starts to weep. Stanley embraces and comforts her. He assures her that Blanche's departure will set things right once more. They'll make love using the colored lights again, and they'll make all the noise they want.

Suddenly, you hear Steve and Eunice's shrieking laughter upstairs. It serves as a reminder that Elysian Fields is a type of jungle, where primitive impulses and instincts prevail.

To bring the so-called party to an end, Stanley presents Blanche with a birthday gift. Blanche perks up in surprise, but when she sees that it's a bus ticket to Laurel, she gags in anguish. Can you find any justification for Stanley's cruelty? However you view Stanley, he seems determined to drag Blanche's life to a tragic conclusion.

As the scene ends, Stella's labor begins, and Stanley rushes her to the hospital.

SCENE NINE

Later that evening Blanche is drinking alone. "The Varsouviana" in the background suggests that she is thinking about her past.

Mitch arrives, unshaven and dressed in work clothes. This is a Mitch you haven't seen before. Blanche quickly hides the bottle. You can tell that he's ready to accuse Blanche of deceiving him. Why he needs to do so is puzzling.

Gruffly, he ignores her offer of a kiss and turns down a drink. Although Blanche is slightly drunk, she's not unaware that Mitch is troubled. As her tension mounts, the music playing in her mind intensifies. Mitch can't hear it, of course, and thinks only that Blanche has drunk too much.

Mitch accuses her of "lapping up [liquor] all summer." Then he startles her by forcing her to turn on a bright light. "I don't think I ever seen you in the light," he says. To get a good look at her, Mitch tears the paper lantern off the light bulb. If you recall that he mounted the lantern on the night they met, what does its removal probably symbolize?

Mitch charges Blanche with deceit. She protests vigorously, preferring to call her misrepresentations "magic." She says, "I don't tell truth, I tell what *ought* to be truth." Clearly, Blanche and Mitch view the world differently. To Blanche illusions are harmless fabrications that make her feel young and alluring. However, Mitch, like Stanley, can't distinguish between illusion and deceit.

NOTE: If Blanche is a tragic figure, she needs a tragic flaw, a quality of personality that leads to her destruction. Ordinarily the flaw may be rather harmless; it might even be admirable. But because of the circumstances in which the tragic figure finds himself, the flaw is lethal. With this in mind, you can probably infer Blanche's tragic flaw from her dialogue with Mitch.

Blanche tries to defend against Mitch's charges by lying. Earlier Blanche won his sympathy with the woeful tale of her marriage. Now she tries to sway him with the next chapter of her heartbreaking story. She explains why she had become intimate with strangers.

Suddenly, they are interrupted by the calls of a

blind Mexican vendor, selling funeral flowers made of tin. Frightened, Blanche tells the uncomprehending Mexican that death led to loss of Belle Reve and to the decline of her happiness and love. She begins to repeat confusing fragments of conversations from her past. The opposite of death, she says, is desire. To prove that she had not been warped by death, she gave herself to young soldiers stationed near Belle Reve. Some might call her action degrading and immoral. Blanche saw it as an affirmation of life.

NOTE: Some critics think that Blanche seems too delicate to have been the whore for a company of soldiers. On the contrary, say other critics. Because Blanche is loving and sensitive, she reacted vehemently to her husband's death. It took a monstrous act to fill her vast emptiness. Her nightly intimacies with soldiers, therefore, are fully understandable.

Unmoved or possibly bewildered by Blanche's tale, Mitch declares that he wants Blanche to give what she's denied him all summer—her body. Only if he'll marry her, she protests. Disgusted, Mitch says that Blanche isn't clean enough to bring into the same house as his mother. He advances, intent on raping her. To scare him off Blanche rushes to the window shouting, "Fire! Fire! Fire!" as Mitch runs off.

SCENE TEN

Blanche is left alone and without hope. A weaker person might do away with herself. But Blanche is likely to find a way out, perhaps in her fantasy world. When this scene opens you find Blanche talking aloud to herself about a moonlight swim in a rock quarry. Is she drunk? Or has her mind become unhinged? You can't be sure until Stanley comes in.

First she asks about Stella. The baby hasn't come yet, so Stanley will spend the night at home. Blanche suddenly becomes wary, alarmed at the thought of being alone in the apartment with him.

He asks about her fine attire. Blanche explains that Shep Huntleigh has invited her on a Caribbean yacht cruise. Stanley plays along with Blanche's fantasy, asking questions and implying that Shep may want more than just Blanche's companionship. She objects and starts to lecture him on the transitory nature of physical things. What lasts, she says is "beauty of the mind and richness of the spirit and tenderness of the heart." To some extent these words may define a philosophy of life that Blanche has unsuccessfully tried to live by. On second thought, perhaps you can find evidence that supports Blanche's partial success.

She stops short, realizing that she's casting pearls before swine—wasting her words on someone who can't appreciate them. Stanley bristles at the word "swine," but holds his tongue. Not for long, however, for when Blanche tells how she has put Mitch in his place for being cruel to her, Stanley explodes in anger. As Stanley's temper builds, Blanche senses danger. To emphasize her terror, stage lighting suddenly engulfs the room in long dancing shadows and lurid reflections. Blanche rushes to the phone to call Shep for help. Meanwhile Stanley retreats to the bathroom to don his special silk pajamas.

He comes out barechested, and grinning. His threatening words cause Blanche to smash a bottle on the table edge and use the jagged top to fend him off. Stanley is excited by the prospect of rough-housing with Blanche. He approaches her cautiously. When she swings at him, he catches her wrist and forces her to drop the weapon. She collapses at his feet. Then he picks up her limp form and carries her into the bedroom.

Is there any reason for Stanley to rape Blanche? Is he a savage or a rapist at heart? Or does he only want to cap his victory over Blanche with this ultimate act of degradation? Rape is such a complex and violent crime that it's usually not easy to identify the motives, although they are worth thinking about.

You might ask who is the winner in the end? And the answer might well be both—Stanley because he achieved gratification: sex, even though it was rape; and Blanche, because she did not submit to her baser instincts and had to be raped.

SCENE ELEVEN

Blanche, of course, has told Stella about the rape. As a new mother, Stella looks to the future with hope and refuses to believe Blanche's story. At the start of this scene Stella tells Eunice, "I couldn't believe her story and go on living with Stanley." Eunice concurs: "Don't ever believe it. Life has got to go on. No matter what happens, you've got to keep on going."

Even if Stella and Eunice secretly believe Blanche's story—you can't tell whether they do or don't—they've chosen to deny its validity. Stella has prob-

ably convinced herself that Blanche invented the
rape to avoid going back to Laurel. Also, after Mitch
threw her off, Blanche lost touch with reality, so
Stella has arranged a "rest" for Blanche at an insane asylum in the country. Some critics have observed that Stella sends Blanche away as an act of
revenge for all the abuse she's taken from her older
sister. On the other hand, Stella may have Blanche's
best interests in mind.

Blanche has confused her trip to the country with
the cruise on Shep's yacht, and as this scene opens,
Blanche is preparing her wardrobe. Stella caters to
Blanche's every wish, hoping to keep her sister
calm before she leaves. She's also feeling remorse-
ful about having committed Blanche to an asylum.
When the time comes for Blanche to be taken away,
Stella cries out in despair. Perhaps she still harbors
doubts about the alleged rape.

During this scene Stanley and his friends are
back at the poker table. This time Stanley is winning. It seems fitting that he should be ahead. This
is the day he resumes his position as king of his
castle.

Blanche's voice diverts Mitch's attention from the
game. You can't be sure what Mitch is thinking,
but his gaze is preoccupied, as though he's pon-
dering what might have been.

Soon the car from the asylum arrives. When
Blanche sees that the doctor is not Shep Huntleigh,
she returns to the apartment, pretending to have
forgotten something. The matron follows and prepares a straitjacket in case Blanche balks or grows
violent. Distressed, Blanche begins to hear voices
as reverberating echoes. Then you hear the polka
playing in the distance. The same lurid reflections

you saw on the night of the rape begin to dance on the apartment walls.

NOTE: All through the play Williams has used sound and light to focus attention on something he wants you to remember. It is a technique you'll find in the works of other American playwrights, like Eugene O'Neill and Thornton Wilder. The montage of images sweeping across the stage in this scene of *Streetcar* demonstrates how vividly the technique can portray characters' emotions.

Stanley and the matron approach Blanche, who becomes increasingly panic-stricken. Stanley tells her cruelly that she hasn't forgotten anything of value unless she means the paper lantern, which he tears off the lightbulb and hands to her. Blanche cries out as if the lantern were herself. She tries to run, but the matron grabs her. Outside, Stella moans, "Oh, God, what have I done to my sister?"

Finally the doctor speaks kindly. Blanche responds with relief and takes his arm. While being escorted to the waiting car, she tells the doctor, "Whoever you are—I have always depended on the kindness of strangers."

Stella is distraught. Stanley comes to her aid. As Blanche is driven away, Stanley puts his hand inside Stella's blouse. It appears that life will soon return to normal for the Kowalskis and for the other residents of Elysian Fields.

A STEP BEYOND

Test and Answers

TEST

1. Blanche proposes that Stella and she escape _____
   from Elysian Fields because Blanche
   A. feels threatened by the lifestyle of the
      place
   B. knows that her younger sister feels
      trapped by the circumstances of life
   C. wants company when she leaves New
      Orleans

2. When Blanche calls Mitch her "Rosenka- _____
   valier," she is
   A. trying to impress him with her
      knowledge of opera
   B. poking fun at his awkwardness
   C. having a bit of harmless fun

3. Mitch asks Blanche why she attempted to _____
   enjoy their date even though she didn't feel
   like it. His question
   I. shows that Mitch is naive
   II. reveals that Mitch does not
       understand Blanche's values
   III. illustrates the clash of cultures you
        find in the play
   A. I and III only   B. II and III only
   C. I, II, and III

4. Stanley feels obliged to tell Mitch about _____
   Blanche's degenerate past because he

   A. wants to destroy Blanche's chance to
      marry Mitch
   B. doesn't want his old army buddy to
      be fooled
   C. will feel guilty if he doesn't

5. In addition to being the name of a streetcar,   ——
   "Desire"
   A. refers to the love between Mitch and
      Blanche
   B. symbolizes the life force in Blanche
      and other characters
   C. stands for Blanche's self-destructive
      personality

6. Blanche tells the truth about   ——
   A. the loss of Belle Reve
   B. her activities in the hotel called
      Tarantula Arms
   C. Shep Huntleigh

7. Stanley can't abide Blanche because   ——
   I. she interferes with his sex life
   II. she considers herself superior to him
   III. of her numerous pretenses
   A. I and II only   B. II and III only
   C. I, II and III

8. Elysian Fields is often called a jungle and   ——
   its residents described in animal terms
   largely because
   A. the play is full of violence
   B. the language of the play reflects
      Blanche's point of view
   C. it's a dangerous place to be

9. Mitch and Blanche are attracted to each other   ——
   because both

   I. have been in love with people who
      died
  II. feel out of place in the brutal world
     around them
III. are lonely and in need of love
  A. I and III only   B. II and III only
  C. I, II, and III

10. Blanche is committed to an asylum at the   _____
    end of the play
    A. to symbolize the victory of brutality
       over gentility
    B. as poetic justice for her sinful life
    C. to keep her safe from further harm

11. In which ways is the conflict between Stanley and
    Blanche more than a mere disagreement between
    two incompatible people?

12. How does Tennessee Williams create the mood for
    Streetcar?

13. How does Stella try to bridge the gap between
    Blanche and Stanley?

ANSWERS

1. A   2. C   3. C   4. A   5. B   6. A
7. C   8. B   9. A   10. A

11. The question implies that Stanley and Blanche are
symbolic figures. Your task is to determine what each
stands for.

   You know that Stanley is lusty and animalistic. He
rages and grunts, but isn't he more than just an uncaged
ape? Outside the house, he holds a responsible job at a
factory. He travels a good deal and apparently earns
enough money to provide for Stella and even to feed

and support Blanche for several months. What does Stanley like to do? He bowls, plays cards, and drinks. If television had been in use in the 1940s, he probably would watch ballgames and sitcoms. Except for his violent streak, he's probably not very much different from millions of other middle-class urban men.

Does Williams mean to imply that Stanley symbolizes middle-class America? Or do Stanley's actions merely suggest that life in that level of society brings out men's basest, most animal-like instincts?

Stanley's adversary, Blanche, represents another stratum of society altogether. Her people used to be wealthy landowners. In the early days, the DuBois family probably owned slaves. Blanche herself is well-educated and appreciates poetry and music. During much of the play she tries to maintain the illusion that traditional values are alive and well. In the end, she is destroyed.

What conclusion might be drawn? That Stanley's world now dominates Blanche's? That Blanche stands for a faded and useless way of life? That man's bestial instincts, repressed by civilization, will again reign supreme? Obviously, the conflict between Stanley and Blanche may be interpreted in many ways. Regardless of how you see it, you can feel certain that it is more than just a misunderstanding between two people who don't see eye to eye.

12. Before you tackle this question, decide what moods you found in the play. "Mood" is an elusive term. A piece of literature as complex as *Streetcar* might contain several moods simultaneously.

Here are some possibilities: (1) violent, angry, and tense; (2) sad and sentimental; (3) sexual and animalistic; (4) morbid and tragic; (5) grotesquely comical. Williams creates such moods using characters' words and actions as well as music, lighting and stage directions. The "Characters" section of this *Book Notes* provides numerous examples of how dialogue and action shape the mood of the play. For example, Stanley's bellowing into the night for Stella to return to him creates a sense of savagery that hangs in the air throughout the play.

If you examine Williams' stage directions, you'll discover prescriptions for mood-enhancing sound effects (trains, voices in the background, gunshots) and music (a waltz for romance, a faint polka to convey the feeling of lost happiness). Similarly, the stage lighting, from the dim glow of Blanche's lanterns to the oppressive glare around the poker table, helps to set the mood of each scene. Williams leaves little to chance. He knows how to create moods and gives play directors plenty of help.

13. It takes skill to mediate between two people who detest each other. If you've ever tried, you can appreciate the problem Stella faces throughout the play. She employs various tactics to force Stanley and Blanche into peaceful coexistence. None of her methods work, however.

From the beginning she pleads for understanding. To keep Blanche from being shocked, Stella prepares her sister to meet Stanley. She explains that Stanley may be different from the sort of men Blanche may be accustomed to. Later, Stella points out Stanley's attractiveness, especially in bed, but her words fall on deaf ears.

Similarly, Stella can't convince Stanley to accept Blanche. He is unmoved by Blanche's delicate condition and the tragic loss of her husband. He distrusts Blanche the moment he meets her. Once he's made up his mind, nothing can sway him.

During most of the play Stella acts as a buffer between the adversaries. Gradually, she drifts toward Blanche's side. Her sister needs help. But if Stella isn't careful, she stands to antagonize Stanley.

Ultimately she sends her sister away. Why Stella sides with Stanley in the end is worth exploring. What has Stella realized about her sister, about Stanley, and about herself? Why can't she simply continue to serve as intermediary? What might Williams be saying by having Stella and Stanley reunited at the end of the play?

Term Paper Ideas and other Topics for Writing

Characters

1. How real are the play's characters? To what degree are they grotesques or caricatures of real people?

2. What are the sources of conflict between Stanley and Blanche? In what ways does the nature of their conflict change as the play progresses?

3. In what ways are Stanley and Blanche symbolic figures?

4. How does each character contribute to Blanche's breakdown? What does Blanche contribute herself?

5. Regardless of her past, why is Blanche a generally sympathetic figure? Explain.

The Meaning of the Play

1. Do the themes in the play have contemporary relevance? In what ways?

2. Is Williams' portrayal of the world totally pessimistic, or does he leave room for at least a little optimism? Defend your answer.

3. Does Williams prefer Blanche's world of traditional Southern gentility or Stanley's of modern hedonism? What is your evidence?

The Play as Drama

1. How does the setting contribute to the mood and meaning of the play?

2. What kinds of symbols does Williams insert in his play, and what does symbolism add to the play's mood or meaning?

3. In which ways does the use of sound contribute to the mood of the play?

4. How does *Streetcar* compare to a classical Greek tragedy?

The Glass Menagerie
&
A Streetcar Named Desire

Further Reading

Durham, Frank. "Tennessee Williams, Theater Poet in Prose." In Parker, *Twentieth Century Interpretations of* The Glass Menagerie, pp. 121–34. A discussion of the play as a type of poem.

Jackson, Esther M. *The Broken World of Tennessee Williams.* Madison: University of Wisconsin Press, 1965. A study of Williams' use of non-realism.

Miller, Jordan Y., editor. *Twentieth Century Interpretations of* A Streetcar Named Desire. Englewood Cliffs: Prentice-Hall, 1971. A rich selection of essays about *Streetcar* as a movie, as a Broadway production, and as a work of dramatic art.

Nelson, Benjamin. "The Play is Memory." In *Tennessee Williams, the Man and his Work.* New York: Ivan Obolensky, Inc., 1961, pp. 98–112. Insightful discussion of characters and themes in *The Glass Menagerie.*

Parker, R. B., editor. *Twentieth Century Interpretations of* The Glass Menagerie. Englewood Cliffs: Prentice-Hall, 1983. A collection of writings about the play, including reviews of the original production.

Rader, Dotson. *Tennessee: Cry of the Heart.* Garden City: Doubleday, 1985. A personal memoir of Williams.

Spoto, Donald. *The Kindness of Strangers.* Boston: Little, Brown, 1985. Deals with Williams' life and art.

Stanton, Stephen, S., editor. *Tennessee Williams: A Collection of Critical Essays.* Englewood Cliffs: Prentice-Hall, 1977. Several essays about Williams, the man, and his plays. One interpretive essay specifically on *The Glass Menagerie.*

Stein, Roger B. "*The Glass Menagerie* Revisited: Catastrophe without Violence." In Stanton, Stephen S., editor, *Tennessee Williams: A Collection of Critical Essays,* pp. 36–44. Fascinating study of the Christian symbolism in the play.

Tharpe, Jac. *Tennessee Williams: Thirteen Essays.* Jackson: University Press of Mississippi, 1980. Critical essays on Williams' work.

Williams, Tennessee. *Memoirs.* New York: Doubleday and Co., 1975. To know the man you must read this autobiography.

AUTHOR'S MAJOR WORKS

1940	*Battle of Angels*
1944	*The Glass Menagerie*
1947	*A Streetcar Named Desire*
1948	*Summer and Smoke*
1950	*The Roman Spring of Mrs. Stone*
1951	*The Rose Tattoo*
1953	*Camino Real*
1955	*Cat on a Hot Tin Roof*
1957	*Orpheus Descending*
1959	*Suddenly Last Summer* (screenplay)
1959	*Sweet Bird of Youth*
1960	*The Fugitive Kind* (screenplay)
1960	*Period of Adjustment*
1961	*The Night of the Iguana*
1963	*The Milk Train Doesn't Stop Here Anymore*
1973	*Small Craft Warnings*

The Critics

On Symbolism in *The Glass Menagerie*

Roger B. Stein thinks that Williams wanted his play to be more than a social and personal tragedy. To suggest the story's deeper meaning, he crowded *The Glass Menagerie* with Christian symbols.

> Amanda, who condemns instinct and urges Tom to think in terms of the mind and spirit, as "Christian adults" do, is often characterized in Christian terms. Her music . . . is "Ave Maria." As a girl, she could only cook angel food cake. She urges Laura, "Possess your soul in patience," and then speaks of her dress for the dinner scene as "resurrected" from a trunk. Her constant refrain to Tom is "Rise an' Shine," and she sells subscriptions to her friends by waking them early in the morning and then sympathizing with them as "Christian martyrs."
>
> . . . In a very real sense both Amanda and Laura are searching for a Savior who will come to help them, to save them, to give their drab lives meaning.
>
> —"*The Glass Menagerie* Revisited:
> Catastrophe without Violence," 1964.

On the Use of Time in *The Glass Menagerie*

The lives of the characters are touched by the past, present, and future. But as critic Frank Durham points out, time is used in a poetic way, too:

> Tom stands with us in the immediate present. . . . But through his consciousness we are carried back in time to his life in the drab apartment before his

escape. . . . Within this train of memory there are two types of time, the generalized and the specific, and through the use of these two we are given a deeper insight into the lives and relationships of the Wingfields. The first scene in the apartment, the dinner scene, is an example of generalized time. It is not any one particular dinner but a kind of abstraction of all the dinners shared by the trio in their life of entrapment. . . .

—"Tennessee Williams, Theater Poet in Prose," 1971

On *A Streetcar Named Desire*

Some early theatergoers were attracted to *A Streetcar Named Desire* by its sensationalism. Others objected to its sordidness. Here is part of theater critic Brooks Atkinson explanation of the artistry of the play:

As a matter of fact, people do appreciate it thoroughly. They come away from it profoundly moved and also in some curious way elated. For they have been sitting all evening in the presence of truth, and that is a rare and wonderful experience. Out of nothing more esoteric than interest in human beings, Mr. Williams has looked steadily and wholly into the private agony of one lost person. He supplies dramatic conflict by introducing Blanche to an alien environment that brutally wears on her nerves. But he takes no sides in the conflict. He knows how right all the characters are—how right she is in trying to protect herself against the disaster that is overtaking her, and how right the other characters are in protecting their independence, for her terrible needs cannot be fulfilled. There is no solution except the painful one Mr. Williams provides in his last scene.

—" 'Streetcar' Tragedy—Mr. Williams' Report on Life in New Orleans," *The New York Times,* 1947

George Jean Nathan, another respected theater critic, found less to admire in *Streetcar*:

> The borderline between the unpleasant and the disgusting is . . . a shadowy one, as inferior playwrights have at times found out to their surprise and grief. Williams has managed to keep his play wholly in hand. But there is, too, a much more shadowy borderline between the unpleasant and the enlightening, and Williams has tripped over it, badly. While he has succeeded in making realistically dramatic such elements as sexual abnormality, harlotry, perversion, seduction and lunacy, he has scarcely contrived to distil from them any elevation and purge. His play as a consequence remains largely a theatrical shocker which, while it may shock the emotions of its audience, doesn't in the slightest shock them into any spiritual education.
>
> —"The Streetcar Isn't Drawn by Pegasus," *The New York Journal-American,* 1947

Imagery in *A Streetcar Named Desire*

Much of the verbal and theatrical imagery that constitutes the drama is drawn from games, chance and luck.... . Indeed, the tactics and ceremonial games in general, and poker in particular, may be seen as constituting the informing structural principle of the play as a whole. Pitting Stanley Kowalski, the powerful master of Elysian Fields against Blanche DuBois, the ineffectual ex-mistress of Belle Reve, Williams makes the former the inevitable winner of the game whose stakes are survival in the kind of world the play posits.

> —Leonard Quirino, "The Cards Indicate a Voyage on A Streetcar Named Desire," *Tennessee Williams: Thirteen Essays,* 1980.